SEAFARERS' VOICES 4

Landsman Hay

LANDSMAN HAY

The Memoirs of Robert Hay

Edited with an introduction by
Vincent McInerney

Seaforth
PUBLISHING

This edition copyright © A Vincent McInerney 2010

First published in Great Britain in 2010 by
Seaforth Publishing,
Pen & Sword Books Ltd,
47 Church Street,
Barnsley S70 2AS

www.seaforthpublishing.com

British Library Cataloguing in Publication Data
A catalogue record for this book is available
from the British Library
ISBN 978 1 84832 068 0

Typeset and designed by M.A.T.S. Leigh-on-Sea, Essex
Printed and bound in Great Britain by
CPI Antony Rowe, Chippenham, Wiltshire

Contents

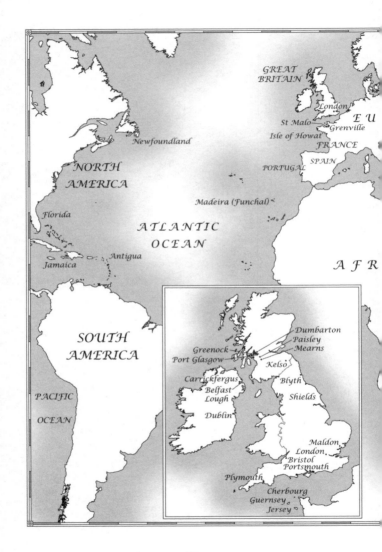

Editorial Note

THE TEXT REFERRED TO in the introductory discussion is *Landsman Hay: Memoirs of Robert Hay*, published by Rupert Hart-Davis in 1953 (and reprinted in 1958), edited by Hay's great-granddaughter, Mavis Doriel Hay from an unidentified source, but presumably a manuscript in the family's possession. The original memoirs were written between September 1820 and November 1821. Some seven years after completing them Hay used some of the material for a series of articles for the *Paisley Magazine*, published under the nom de plume 'Sam Spritsail'. In these articles Hay also included material not found in the original *Memoirs*, and in the 1953 edition, M D Hay gives this added material as passages in italics within the volume.

In this 2010 edited abridgement all the material, original and italicised, has been melded to form one inclusive narrative. The word count has been reduced from about 55,000 to 45,000, mainly as a result of a reduction in repetition, although also with some simplification for the sake of clarity. Having said this, there are times when Hay's vivid and dramatic style is exactly suited to the subject immediately under discussion, as for example, his evocation of 'the pestiferous breaths and pestilential vapours of the press room.'

Introduction

> Our fleets, which are defrauded by injustice, are first
> manned by violence and maintained by cruelty.
>   Admiral Edward Vernon[1]

IN THE FIRST THREE volumes of Seafarer's Voices we
heard from Jean Marteilhe, a galley slave, George
Shelvocke, an impecunious privateer, and John Newton,
a sometime slaving captain who went on to pen what
eventually became the hymn 'Amazing Grace'. All of
these were from solid, professional backgrounds, and
were active in the first three-quarters of the eighteenth
century. With this fourth volume, the *Memoirs* of Robert
Hay (1789-1847), we come to an account of service on
the lower deck of the Royal Navy during the great
French wars – Hay was at sea from 1803 to 1811 – with
a narrator coming from a more humble background,
Hay's family being essentially Scottish weavers and
textile workers.

First-hand accounts of life in the Navy of Nelson's
time are surprisingly common, even from among the
ranks of ordinary seamen, but they were mostly written

late in life, when social mores had changed, and historians have argued that their views were untypical: the very fact that they were literate set them apart from the norm of shipboard attitudes. The darker side of British naval life – the 'press gang', ferocious discipline and harsh conditions – have become a hot topic of debate among social historians, but in general the old Victorian view of the Navy, epitomised by John Masefield's claim that its success was 'built up by the blood and agony of thousands of barbarously maltreated men', no longer holds sway.[2] Hay offers a unique insight into these issues: he was very young when he first went to sea and his account was written not many years after (originally without, apparently, an eye to publication); furthermore, he was not 'pressed' but volunteered, although he soon chose to desert, and was later pressed back into the Navy. In this, and in the very mixed treatment he received at the hands of his superiors, Hay's experience was probably typical of many naval seamen's careers, but what makes Hay's account rare, if not unique, is his depiction of the life of a boy servant – the 'cabin boy' of public imagination, although Hay refers to himself as 'shoe boy'[3] – a juvenile rating allotted to, or chosen by, an officer's personal servant. This unusual viewpoint makes for an interesting, and credible, picture of lower-deck life in the British Navy of that time.

Robert Hay was born in Dumbarton in 1789. At that

time his father, a weaver, had taken over a farm, but being unable to meet an increase in rent demanded by the landlord, he went back into the clothing trade. As a child Hay learned to read early, though he claims that his writing abilities did not keep pace. In his memoirs he does not discuss any books, except *Robinson Crusoe*, wishing he could have been Crusoe's 'companion'. In order to give himself the opportunity of perhaps embracing this role for some other abandoned mariner, he left the family home early one morning in 1803 to walk to Greenock to look for a ship. Like much in the book, this leaving home is recounted in a matter of fact style but Hay makes an effort to recreate his state of mind and motivation at the time – Hay states that he wrote his memoirs to give his children an idea of his early years, and he is often explicit about the lessons he has learned from life.

At Greenock, Hay fell in with two other boys seeking sea employment, and under their aegis he ended up at the naval 'rendezvous', the place (often an inn) where the press gang set up its headquarters in any given town. With the Navy of this era desperate for man-power, the press rendezvous, or 'rondy', was the equivalent of an astronomical black hole – once inside its gravitational pull there was no escape. However, at this point in his career Hay desired no escape, so he joined up willingly, and was sent to a press tender 'a mile or two from shore' while waiting to be transported south to Plymouth or Portsmouth. However, his father traced him, and came aboard the tender to try to gain his son's freedom. The amount of money needed to buy Hay's freedom was beyond the pockets of the family – Hay does not explain the detail, but if it were a question of refunding the volunteer's 'bounty', this would be understandable as it was the equivalent to about five years' wages for a seaman.[4] Just before Hay sailed for Plymouth, his father and sister returned to give him a Bible, a set of seaman's clothing, and some advice on future conduct. This was last time Hay was to hear his father's voice, the latter dying while Hay was still at sea.

Hay eventually reached Plymouth in August 1803 and went through the Navy's induction process, being put first aboard the examination ship *Resolu*, and then the guard ship *Salvador del Mundo*, a Spanish three-decker taken by the fleet of 'Hanging' Admiral Jervis at the Battle of Cape St Vincent in 1797. Hay's description of life aboard the *Salvador del Mundo* in 1803 is not one of horror, but he was pleased to leave it for his next ship, the *Eling*. He tells us of bosun's mates and their canes chasing the 'people' (the crew) up and down various hatches in an attempt to get the decks and ship cleaned; the permanent crew and their extended families using the lower deck as a sort of retail 'cash and carry', and attempting to smuggle aboard gin and rum.

There is, however, another description of the *Salvador del Mundo* from this period that presents a different picture altogether – the account of impressment left by Charles Reece Pemberton (1790-1840) in *Pel Verjuice*. Pemberton was born in a labourer's cottage in Pontypool in 1790, 'cabbages being more abundant than carnations',[5] but the family moved to Birmingham where Pemberton grew up a sensitive and unusually angst-ridden youth besotted by poetry and drama. His romantic nature eventually got the better of him, and he decided to run away to sea with a friend, George.

Pemberton describes how in 1806 – three years later than Hay joined – they were roaming Liverpool docks, eyeing 'with delight' the many boards suspended in the rigging of ships announcing their destinations, when they noticed 'two well-dressed sailors . . . clean . . . white-trowsered . . . abundant-buttoned . . . glazed-hatted . . . quid-cheeked . . . pigtailed', who walked wherever they walked. These two told Pemberton that their ship was better than either boy has yet seen, with 'a jolly captain who splices the main-brace every week' and who would 'order the pusser's steward to blow your kite out with lobscous and choke your luff with figgy-dowdy.'[6] These sailors escorted the boys to the press rendezvous where they were persuaded into joining the Navy by 'a very handsome man, with an epaulette on each shoulder – and armless sleeve dangling from one'.

Pemberton and George were removed to the tender
Friendship, where they were shocked by the first
realisation of what they were amongst: 'Eight or ten
men, with hard, rugged, weather-beaten faces', and on
the forecastle 'as many more squalid, dirty-bearded,
matted-haired wretches, stockingless and shoeless, with
enormous splay-feet. The wildest creatures I have ever
looked upon. And what faces! Each carried a
countenance of reckless misery, a hatred of hope.'
While locked under a grating in the hold, Pemberton
saw 'A crowded mass of disgusting and fearful heads
and trunks, bundled and scattered, laughing scream-
ing, cursing and fighting ... The offscourings of
villainy and the jails', but also 'men whose lives and
characters were unimpeachable . . . forcibly seized from
their hearth-sides', and others taken after years at sea
as their merchant ships re-entered British waters. 'All',
Pemberton tells us, were 'mingled in a pestiferous den',
every morning emptied of its inanimate filth, 'except
that glued and engrained to the bodies of its occupants.
Old England's jolly tars, men who sing "Britons never,
never, never, will be slaves."'

Pemberton had no illusions, commenting: 'these men
were the right sort to be ruled by the "privileged" ...
What would become of the Navy if its seamen were
instructed to think, or allowed to reason? ... Their
daring intrepidity would dwindle into calculation, the
reckless bravery evaporate into foresight and caution.'

Pemberton's companion George, unable to cope with his circumstances, decided to swim the mile and a half to shore, and was eventually found entwined in a brig's cable, half-eaten by fishes.

When he reached Portsmouth, Pemberton was transferred to Hay's *Salvador del Mundo* where he fell foul of the bosun's mates and their 'colts' – knotted ropes used for beating a man. Pemberton memorably describes this casual form of punishment:

> I received one of the blows across my shoulders which sent the blood at once whizzing and boiling back upon my heart; seeming to fall through my bones into my breast, so ponderous was the stroke. I reeled, and became sick and faint; this gave him the opportunity of repeating the blow, as if it were too delicious a pleasure to be lost; my limbs bowed under me and I sank on the deck, senseless. . . . I do not know who, or how many, trampled on me . . . but I do remember that an hour after I had recovered, there was a drumming in my ears, and my brain seemed to be compressed between hard bandages, and a hoop of iron was welded round my brow and I stood in a stupor gazing down towards the deck, *trying to look at something that was not there.* Thank God, I have thought a hundred times since, there was no knife within my reach, or I am sure I should have driven it into his heart.

He was beaten senseless by the same man the next day. Pemberton points out that although they would have hanged him for murder had he stayed on that ship, mature reflection has made him see that it was not the bosun's mate who was to blame but the 'system he had been taught by'.[7] Pemberton's final thoughts are that it is not only his own tale he is telling, but that of thousands who have had no historian. He adds that 'palpable cruelty makes no impression if gently breathed', and that 'words must be strong, or else the picture will not be seen.'

Pemberton, of course, was an unusual sort of man to find on the lower deck of a warship, and although he served until he was twenty-four (1806-1812), he then made better use of his theatrical personality when he became an actor-manager in the West Indies. He married, but left his wife after she began an affair with a local governor, and the remainder of his life was dogged by bad luck and ill-health. Nowadays Pemberton's writings are almost unknown, and are perhaps too highly coloured to be useful to maritime historians, but they do form a notable contrast with Hay's more prosaic view of his lot.

Hay's time on the *Salvador del Mundo* ended when he was transferred to the schooner *Eling* in August 1803. Life in minor warships was always different; discipline tended to be less formal, and the small crew often formed a close bond. Hay became a favourite among the crew and was taught some basic seamanship, but this seems to have gone to his head, so when he overheard that he was getting spoilt he resolved to become more affable and modest, a ploy which served him throughout the rest of his naval career.[8] Although he expressed no unhappiness about life in the schooner, when the *Eling* returned to Plymouth for a refit Hay saw the chance to 'run' – desert – but after failing to find a berth on a merchant vessel he had to return to his own ship. No reason is given for his decision to desert: the chance occurs and Hay immediately takes it but, unlike Pemberton, he does not reveal his thinking. Hay may have felt such matters were of no interest to – or no business of – the family he wrote for, but he probably felt it was a sensitive issue and indeed, as we shall see later, one which returned to haunt him.

Hay transferred to the *Culloden* (74 guns), where he became a boy servant of a Lieutenant Hawkins – 'a kind and indulgent master'[9] – Hay's duty being to make sure Hawkins was sprucely turned out, to maintain Hawkins' cabin, and to stand behind the lieutenant's chair in the wardroom to make sure Hawkins received his share of 'the good things going at the table'. There was also, of course, a counter-obligation on Hawkins: to be his servant, Hay must be dressed and fed properly, otherwise this would reflect badly on Hawkins himself. Hay would now, in a sense, be socially removed from the other boy seamen and be given limited entrée into a world far removed from a Scots weaver's cottage. Hay had access to Hawkins' cabin and personal effects and nautical instruments; Hay used the opportunity to try to master the quadrant using a lighted candle on Hawkins' dresser in place of the sun.

Admiral Collingwood, well known for his enlightened concern for the welfare of his crews, hoisted his flag on the *Culloden* and seemed to regard Hay favourably. It was Collingwood's practice to improve the nautical competence of each boy by putting them under the charge of the best seaman of the mess to which that boy belonged, and accordingly Hay was assigned to Jack Gillies: according to Hay a gifted polymath who could do everything but write.

In 1804 the *Culloden* sailed for the East Indies under a new admiral, Rear Admiral Pellew. Hawkins had left the ship, and Hay now served two masters, Mr Dunsterville, the chaplain, and Mr Crease, the master's mate, neither of whom impressed him. Dunsterville he dismissed with the observation: 'The Church of England appears to require less talent and application in its ministers, particularly those appointed to naval service, than that of Scotch Presbyterians.' Crease he described as 'hasty in temper, haughty in demeanour, and arrogant and overbearing in disposition', with 'all the whiffling activity of a Frenchman.'[10] This use of 'whiffling' as applied to Crease is probably a reference to the satirical portrait of Captain Whiffle in Smollett's popular 'naval' novel *Roderick Random* (1748).

Our new commander, Captain Whiffle, came on board in a ten-oared barge, overshadowed with a vast umbrella. A tall, thin, young man, dressed in a white hat garnished with a red feather, from whence his hair flowed in ringlets on his shoulders ... surrounded with a crowd of attendants, all of whom, in their different degrees, seemed of their patron's disposition; and with so many perfumes, that the clime of Arabia Felix was not half so sweet-scented.[11]

In his description of, and his dealing with, Messrs Dunsterville and Crease, we again see the odd position and powers of the lower-deck 'shoe boy'. According to Hay, Dunsterville faithfully kept his promises but was judged by the seamen as mean, their evaluation of a man's goodness being based on the 'liberality by which they distribute spirits' to those who rendered them any little service. Dunsterville also kept Hay 'very bare of pocket money',[12] which was a bigger offence than it might seem, since the officer received the wages of his servant and was expected to use it, largely if not entirely, for that servant's benefit.

Crease promised to increase Hay's stock of clothing, as well as allowing Hay the use of books and pens and paper and to supply Hay with little necessaries for the long voyage. None of these were forthcoming and matters reached such a pass that one evening Hay 'lodged with the captain [Cole] a complaint of his [Crease's] cruelty.' Crease was sent for, and reprimanded in front of a number of other officers and seamen, and told by the captain that as he did not know how to treat a boy he would not have another while he remained in the ship. This is startling – that a lower-deck boy could have a master's mate publicly reprimanded, at a time when for an ordinary seaman (much less a boy) to even look askance at any officer, or petty officer, was to invite severe corporal punishment. But the Navy had strict rules, and Crease was in flagrant breach of them. It is possible that the fourteen-year-old Hay was so sure of his position to feel he could take such a step with every chance of success because he knew his captain's reputation. Cole had spent many years in the eastern seas, and took vigorous measures to preserve the health of his crews in a dangerous climate, so if he felt that Crease's parsimony threatened the well-being of even his most junior ratings, Cole is likely to have made an example of him.

After the ship had arrived in the Indies, Hay injured his ankle at Pulopenang, and when it got worse he was told he would have to lose a leg. However, playing on the Scots connection between himself and the surgeon, Hay dropped a few tears and the surgeon agreed to see what could be done ashore at Madras. Hay spent five months in the naval hospital and, despite the poor reputation of contemporary medicine, emerged partially cured, and still with two legs. He rejoined the *Culloden* to find both Dunsterville and Crease had left, but only after impugning his reputation. Thereafter 'No duty could be more oppressive, no service too vile.'[13] However, the admiral's secretary, Edward Hawke Locker, who had been residing ashore in Madras, took up quarters aboard and chose Hay as his servant. All was transformed in an instant. In a vivid little cameo, Hay describes how he was turning a spit on which a young 'porker' was cooking when the news was made public, the spit handle to leeward, the smoke rolling into Hay's eyes. One of Hay's most assiduous tormentors, a master-at-arms called Young – 'a cruel tyrannical knave' – rushed up to say that he had been trying to procure for Hay a good situation for a long time and had now succeeded. This inveterate enemy gave Hay his handkerchief to wipe his face and then proffered all the services of a true friend. Hay, 'dissembling in my turn', replied in kind.[14]

This illustrates one of the fundamental realities of naval service: patronage, or 'interest' as it was known at the time. From the most senior admiral to the meanest boy servant, career advancement was influenced, if not dominated, by the people you knew and who could promote your interests. Hay's shipboard life could be hell, or heaven, depending on whether anybody further up the hierarchy took him under their wing. And with a powerful patron, even his superiors – like Young – were forced to treat him with respect, or they themselves might suffer from the disapproval of that patron.

Locker (1777-1849) was at this time about twenty-eight and was to have a profound effect on Hay, who tried to emulate him in many ways. He went so far as to mention Locker in the prologue that Hay wrote for a play that was to be performed on board. However, Locker 'gently drew his pen', through the lines which mentioned him.[15] The seamen, too, liked Locker – so much so they took his dog Dasher ashore, 'treating' the animal until it lay drunk under a bar table.

Locker had an extensive library with him and to this Hay was given full access. Locker also ensured Hay got plenty of shore leave, which broadened his outlook and understanding of the world. After a year or two in Indian seas the fleet experienced a want of shipwrights and the *Culloden*'s carpenter, Mr Forbes, suggested Hay train in that branch. Forbes pointed out that it would provide a trade; surely, Forbes asked, he could not wish to be an officer's 'shoe boy' for ever? Hay realised the common sense in this, especially in providing a skill that he would be able to use ashore when he left the Navy. Hay also knew Locker was leaving, and applied to him for release. Typically, Hay did not mention the carpenter's post, simply stating that he wished to be rated as a 'seaman' rather than a 'boy'. Locker agreed, and Hay left his service for the adze and axe.

Between 1806 and 1809 the *Culloden* was engaged against French and Dutch colonies in the East, but the

Culloden's crew also became involved in the mutiny at Vellore. In commenting on this Hay gives us possibly the only political remark he ever makes concerning the British presence in India:

> Once ashore, our marines took over garrison duty, while the garrison soldiers marched inland against the rebels – if rebels they could be called who were fighting to restore their ancient laws and institutions, and wresting the patrimony of their ancestors, from the greedy hands of violent, haughty, and avaricious usurpers.[16]

Hay worked steadily at his carpentering, and in 1809 the ship returned to England via the Cape of Good Hope. After five years of continuous service Hay was given fourteen days' leave and £14 spending money, one-third of his wages for those five years. He left the ship with a close friend, Richard Wright, and tried to make it to Scotland. This plan fell through and the two men ended up sightseeing in London where Hay called on Locker, was kindly received, and presented with two books. The workings of patronage could be enduring, but needed to be consciously cultivated.

Returning to Plymouth Hay was briefly put on the *Salvador del Mundo* again before being transferred to the *Amethyst*, frigate. Operating independently, the *Amethyst* was employed in one of the classic roles of the frigate, reconnoitring the coasts of France, Spain and Portugal, disrupting trade and taking small coasting vessels. Hay joined the carpenter's crew of this vessel which, following a refit at Plymouth, was ready for sea again in February 1811.[17] On the night of the 15th the ship was riding at a single cable in order to make a quick departure the following morning, when a gale came up and the ship began to drag her anchor. The *Amethyst* was driven ashore, but the ship did not break up immediately and Hay was able to escape down a type of early breeches buoy. In the dark and confusion Hay again decided to desert.

He went to the house of some friends and they agreed to hide him, but while he was safe here during the day, there was only one bedroom, so he had to cross the street to his sleeping place every night, with the press always on the watch. Hay could see Plymouth harbour and all its craft passing before his window, and one description he gives of an eponymous 'Jack' ashore – having just returned from a voyage and paid-off – would have been a worthy subject of that Bruegel of the British Navy, Thomas Rowlandson (1756-1827):

> . . . and lastly, the jolly tar himself was seen with his white demity trowsers fringed at the bottom, his fine scarlet waistcoat bound with black ribbon, his dark blue broadcloth jacket studded with pale buttons, his black silk neckcloth thrown carelessly about his sunburnt neck. An elegant hat of straw, indicative of his recent return from a foreign station, cocked on

one side; a head of hair reaching into his waistband;
a smart switch made from the backbone of a shark
under one arm; his doxy under the other, a huge chew
of tobacco in his cheek, and a good throat season of
double stingo recently deposited within his belt by
way of fending off care. Thus fitted out, in good
sailing trim, as he himself styles it, he strides along
with all the importance of an Indian Nabob.[18]

Hay was eventually found a berth by a friendly
waterman on a ship called the *Edward* bound for the
West Indies. However, as Hay's account vividly
portrays, life in the merchant marine was subject to its
own hardships and uncertainties, particularly for
deserters from the King's service. The *Edward* lay near
the wreck of the *Amethyst* and every boat that
approached put Hay on tenterhooks in case it
contained one of the *Amethyst's* officers who might
recognise him. However, a week later the ship sailed
and passed into the open sea without being boarded by
a man-of-war's boat looking for seamen to impress. For
the moment Hay was safe.

Hay made himself particularly useful assisting the
carpenter, who was used only to heavy dockyard work,
but on approaching Jamaica and the advent of yet
another set of man-of-war's boats, the crew once again
faced the danger of impressment into the Navy. Usually
the press was only interested in professional seamen

(and in strict legal terms, their powers were confined to those who made the sea their trade), so Hay 'dressed like a footman, and adopted an air of flippancy', hoping to be mistaken for a steward. Luckily they entered Port Royal at night so his ruse was not put to the test.

At Jamaica almost all of the crew deserted, in circumstances close to mutiny, and such was the dissatisfaction with the master and the state of the ship that two of the crew hailed a warship's boat and volunteered for the Navy. Although merchant seamen were better paid, were not subject to such strict discipline, and were free to return home at the end of a voyage, there were also well-understood disadvantages compared to naval service. The workload was heavier because crews were as small as the owners could get away with; the ships were not always well-found (the leaky state of the *Edward* was a major factor in the desertions); food was often poor; and the crew were still at the mercy of an arbitrary, and sometimes tyrannical, master.

Hay, having cut his foot badly with an adze, could not join the deserters, who included the carpenter, so making the best of the situation Hay accepted the position. However, the tight-fisted master would not pay for a carpenter's warrant in Hay's name – a warrant that would (in theory) exclude its holder from being pressed. Therefore, after a new crew was found and the ship sailed for England in July 1811, Hay was still liable to be pressed. One of the professional sailor's greatest complaints against the system of impressment, which many accepted as a necessary evil, was the Navy's habit of pressing sailors out of returning merchantmen – just as they were looking forward to a run ashore after what could be a voyage of months, if not years, they were effectively kidnapped and sent back to sea for as long as the Navy needed them, a potentially limitless engagement. Merchant ships thus raided were usually left with only enough hands to see them into port.

In Hay's case, when the ship reached Bristol, almost inevitably, they were boarded by the press. Merchant seamen were so used to this that they had evolved their own counter-strategies. The most common was to fashion a 'stow hole' among the cargo, and Hay's was behind some hogsheads of sugar, so when three of the press came below to search – thrusting their cutlasses among the cargo – Hay, fortunately, was far enough back to escape detection. But he still needed to avoid the port, so at about midnight, the second mate, bosun, and Hay offered three half-guineas to a passing boat to land them quietly ashore. This was done although the mate of the *Edward* had to be faced down before he would allow Hay to leave.

They were landed on a deserted patch of coast, but before daybreak reached the village of Pill, where Hay and the second mate were hidden in a priest hole at the inn. In fact, this was probably constructed for smugglers, but was useful during visits from the press. Communities that earning their living from the sea were very sympathetic to the plight of seamen (and smugglers), and could usually be relied upon to help a man escape the press. At this inn Hay met an Irish girl and her parents waiting for 'a fair wind to Cork'. Hay fell in love with her, writing and dedicating a poem to her. When he was finally paid the wages owed him, Hay walked to Bath and took a coach for London, where he arrived in September 1811, intending to take ship back to Scotland.

Nowhere in any 'sailortown' was entirely safe for a seaman, and as he made his way across Tower Hill towards the masts of the 'Scots smacks', he felt 'the tap on the shoulder' and heard the well-known enquiry: 'What ship?' Hay denied any knowledge of shipping, but his questioner gave a whistle and soon Hay was in the hands of six or so of a press gang. He was taken to the 'rondy' and questioned by a lieutenant, where he was soon exposed. Everything in a sailor's demeanour exposed his calling: even if he changed his clothing, his manner of speech, and even his rolling gait marked him out from landlubbers. Hay's particular dread was that they might examine his bundle, which contained clothing with British naval markings – theft of material bearing the King's Broad Arrow could mean death –

but he managed to get rid of these before he was sent
to a receiving ship at Tower Wharf. In the great cabin
he was further questioned and must have given a false
name – what this was has never been ascertained, but
it was common practice, as so many deserters knew no
other trade but the sea, so the chance of being pressed
all over again was very high. This time Hay refused to
sign on, and was taken below as 'a pressed man'.
Bounties for 'volunteers' were reduced as the war went
on, but the fact that Hay thought it not worth going
through the charade probably meant that he had
already made up his mind that he would not be in the
Navy long enough to collect this meagre inducement.

Conditions were as bad, or possibly worse, than on
the *Salvador del Mundo*, and from Tower Wharf they
were taken to the Nore and put aboard the *Ceres*,
guard ship. On this vessel they were given the freedom
of the deck, as it was moored six miles from shore,
which together with a strong tide was considered at
too great a distance to escape. In October 1811 Hay
met John Patterson, a native of Hartley, and the men
gradually struck up a friendship that produced a plan
to escape from the *Ceres*. They obtained some
bladders which they fashioned into inflatable life
preservers that would hold the human body upright in
the water, and in the dark of an October evening,
fortified by a couple of glasses of rum, Hay and
Patterson went over the side on a rope. Steering by

the great comet of 1811 they eventually made land, intending to try for Maldon, Essex, where Patterson knew the captains of various colliers which were bound for the north. It was morning when they reached the Essex shore and Hay described the mood in one of his exuberant wordy bursts:

> The sun was shining in meridian splendour, scarcely a cloud was to be seen in the wide expanse, the mild zephyrs, as they skimmed along the fragrant meadow or over those fields which showed they had recently contributed to the support of man, seemed to whisper congratulations in our ear.[19]

Again the seamen met local sympathy when they called at a farmhouse run by a woman who had a son in the merchant marine, and after reaching Maldon that evening, Hay procured a passage to Sunderland and Patterson to Blyth. Hay slept ashore (presumably to minimise the danger from press gangs) only to find next morning that his ship had sailed, but he was quick to sign on another and worked his passage on a brig bound for Shields. He knew there were four press gangs operative at Shields, and obtained the use of one of the brig's stow holes from the master, but again Hay was lucky in that his ship arrived at night and a great number of vessels crossed the bar at once. Hay let Mrs Patterson know her husband was safe, before continuing on to Scotland and home.

Hay, by now having learned the value of education, persuaded his mother to fund him in navigation, arithmetic and bookkeeping courses. In 1812 the Ardrossan Canal trade began and Hay obtained a place as steersman, and then captain, of one of the trading barges; in 1813 he became clerk and storekeeper. He met his wife to be in autumn 1815 and they married in June 1816. He tells us she 'possessed neither beauty nor fortune' – but adds that neither did he. He ends his *Memoirs* on 6 November 1821, aged thirty-two, seemingly satisfied with life.

Hay's eldest son, John Hay (1819-1843), wrote some reminiscences in which he describes an incident that occurred in 1830. A surgeon friend of the Hay family, William Nisbet, was visiting London and was given an introduction to Locker by Hay. Locker wrote back to Hay offering to sponsor his ten-year-old son John Hay for a place at the Mathematical School of Greenwich Hospital, 'the very best foundation of the kind in Britain' where young John would be 'completely fitted out for the Merchant Service'.[20] Hay must have realised that this meant some official scrutiny of his service record, but eventually agreed the boy's name should be put forward. A letter was then received from Greenwich telling Robert Hay that in the books of the Navy, the letter 'R' (Ran) had been found against his name regarding his flight from the wreck of the *Amethyst* in 1811: that is, Hay was a deserter, and was still officially classed as such. This must have been a blow to both father and son, as Locker's recommendations would have opened many doors.

The latter part of Hay's life led him towards the pursuit of literature – a path he had always wished to tread. The articles mentioned above that he wrote for the *Paisley Magazine* in 1828 attracted the attention of William Motherwell, who edited both the *Magazine* and the *Paisley Advertiser*. In March 1830 Hay became sub-editor of the *Advertiser*, and also acquired an interest in a lithographic and printing business, resigning from the Canal Company after eighteen years' service. Hay became editor seven months later when Motherwell moved on to the *Glasgow Courier*, and retained this post until 1844 when he retired in favour of his second son, Robert Hay the younger. Robert Hay the elder died in 1847 in his fifty-eighth year.

Although a known deserter, Hay was not pursued. The wars were over, and in peacetime the Navy had more voluntary recruits than it needed. Moreover, the sheer scale of desertion in the wartime Navy made concerted legal action beyond contemplation. One contemporary pamphlet calculated that in two years alone from May 1803 to June 1805, at a time when the Navy's nominal strength was around 90,000 seamen, over 12,000 deserted.[21] This may go some way to solving the major puzzle of the memoirs, the two decisions to desert – both without any explanation. Hay never mentions any long-standing resentments and hatreds as such, but when an opportunity presents itself to desert, he embraces it as a matter of course. Professional seamen probably regarded the press, like wind and tide, as an unpredictable but unavoidable feature of their working lives. In Volume 3 of *Seafarers' Voices*, John Newton dismisses his pressing in one sentence (though knowing his father will relieve him); as does Lurting, a century earlier, in the first sentence of his *The Fighting Sailor Turn'd Peaceable Christian*: 'In the Year 1646, I being then about Fourteen Years of Age, was impress'd (or forc'd) and carry'd into the Wars in *Ireland*, where I remained about two Years.'[22] To be taken up was a misfortune, but since they had not joined voluntarily, seamen had little compunction in absconding – and they did so in such large numbers that it was not something that required much explanation.

Hay's time as a 'shoe boy' served him well in later life. The kindness of some of his officers, especially Locker, allowed him to grow and develop. From men like Collingwood, Dunsterville, Crease and Locker, he learned things that a lifetime in the weaving trade could not have given him, and he seems to have personally attracted the attention of those who could best help him, or to whom he made himself amenable. Hay's account of the fluctuating fortunes of so junior a rating are a revelation, and perhaps unique within the literature. When in favour, the pocket money, clothing, access to books and nautical instruments and writing materials that seem to have been his natural expectation, almost a prescriptive right, are surprising. But this is contrasted with his immediate demotion to dogsbody when Dunsterville and Crease leave – followed by his equally swift reinstatement to somebody of note when Locker chooses him as a servant, causing a powerful enemy, the master-at-arms, to immediately begin courting Hay's favour once the news is known.

Like most seafarers of the time, Hay's entire seagoing career was haunted by the spectre of the press, and much of his account is concerned with ways of evading it. He says little about his personal feelings on the subject – simply escaping whenever the opportunity presented – but after the war impress-ment was never again employed, although the laws supporting it were not actually repealed. There was to be no major naval war to require it, but in any event the tide of public opinion had turned firmly against it. Victorian liberals came to see impressment as a legal travesty and morally reprehensible, with damaging social consequences.

The heartbreaking case of Mary Jones was quoted by Charles Dickens in the introduction to his novel *Barnaby Rudge*, and stands as an example of the effects of the press at its most iniquitous, and shows it to be a practice which could readily destroy whole families:

Introduction

That the case of Mary Jones may speak the more emphatically for itself, I subjoin it, as related by SIR WILLIAM MEREDITH in a speech in Parliament, *'On Frequent Executions'*, made in 1777. Under this act [The Shop-lifting Act], one Mary Jones was executed. It was at the time when press warrants were issued, on the alarm about the Falkland Islands. The woman's husband was pressed, their goods seized for some debts of his, and she, with two small children, turned into the streets a-begging. It is a circumstance not to be forgotten, that she was very young (under nineteen), and most remarkably handsome. She went to a linen-draper's shop, took some coarse linen off the counter, and slipped it under her cloak; the shopman saw her, and she laid it down: for this she was hanged. Her defence was (I have the trial in my pocket), 'that she had lived in credit, and wanted for nothing, till a press-gang came and stole her husband; but since then, she had no bed to lie on; nothing to give her children to eat; and they were almost naked; and perhaps she might have done something wrong, for she hardly knew what she did.' The parish officers testified the truth of this story; but it seems, there had been a good deal of shop-lifting about Ludgate; an example was thought necessary; and this woman was hanged for the comfort and satisfaction of shopkeepers in Ludgate Street. When brought to receive sentence, she behaved in such a frantic manner, as proved her mind to be in a distracted and desponding state; and the child was sucking at her breast when she set out for Tyburn.[23]

After this judicial verdict, there may have been those who felt that the government had perhaps acted harshly, even unjustly, in hanging Mary Jones. Fortunately, there were the words of that 'great oracle of law', Lord Mansfield (1705-1793), to reassure them: 'The power of pressing is deduced from that trite maxim of the Constitutional Law of England, that private mischief had better be submitted to than that public detriment should ensue.'[24] Some readers may be more disposed to agree with another Dickensian character who made the famous statement: 'If the law supposes that,' said Mr Bumble, squeezing his hat emphatically in both hands, 'the law is *a* ass . . .'[25]

Landsman Hay

1. Birth and childhood – Renfrew and Paisley: 1789-1803

THE SCENES IN WHICH we ourselves have acted a part often assume in our eyes an importance they by no means possess in the eyes of others. But as these memoirs are intended solely for the inspection of my children, perhaps the reader may be disposed to grant me a certain leniency in what I have to recount. For while the knowledge I possess of my father's history is regrettably scant in the extreme, I intend, by the following sheets, to serve my children in a better fashion. My father was a penetrating, judicious man, though inclined to be hasty in his temper. Prone to secrecy, I do not remember hearing a single anecdote or incident that befell him before his marriage. While his education for his business, the cloth trade, was sufficient, the stock of ornamental learning was limited. Having a large family to care for on the products of his industry, he could afford no time for the cultivation of fine arts.

I was born on 27 October 1789, at the farm of Woodley in the shire of Dumbarton. My grandfather on the paternal side had also occupied this farm. At my grandfather's decease, about the year 1785, my father who, until that time, had followed the weaving business, now took over this farm for the remaining eight years of the lease. My father had married, in 1779, Agnes Calder, whose father was owner of the farm immediately adjoining ours. The adjacency of my mother's people, who were in easy circumstances, might have been of material service to my father and my mother, but my mother had married in opposition to the will of her parents and there existed a degree of coldness between both families.

In 1793, the lease of my father's farm expired, and the rent being demanded on the new lease being nearly double what it was before, my father considered it impossible to realise enough from the farm to cover the increase and therefore gave it up. No other agricultural work appearing, my father sold off his farming implements, and removed to Wellmeadow in the parish of Mearns, Renfrewshire.

In this place bleaching of cloth was carried out by my uncle Robert, for whom my father went to work as a boiler. Our family at this time consisted of nine children, the two eldest alone who could contribute anything by their earnings, one working at embroidering muslin at 3s a week, the other darning with my uncle Robert at 1s 6d. My father's wages being 9s, our total income was 13s 6d a week to support a family of eleven.[26] From the smallness of these resources it will be easily conceived that, to make income and expenditure agree, the most prudent economy was necessary. This virtue my mother possessed in a high degree. She brought no money into the house but once it was there, she showed herself very expert in keeping it from going out. She was equally careful with her time, never allowing one minute to go to waste, and seemed quite rejoiced to supply the child in the cradle with its wants at the commencement of the meal, because then she could, at the same time, also supply her own, and ours. With her own hands she spun the greater part of the family clothing, and even though many a patch bedecked our garments, a single hole was never seen in them, and with our faces washed, our hair combed, and our countenances glowing with health and vigour, we presented a lovely picture of good management and rural happiness.

It was then practice for people to run accounts with grocers for articles of food from one pay day to another, nearly every family being one week behind on goods previously received, so that often, even on pay night, families were forced to take out debts anew. My mother, however, paid ready money for every article she bought, and when the pay came to hand, instead of needing to appropriate it to the liquidation of the debt she was able to deposit it in a drawer to supply any future wants.

It will be supposed by many that from so slender an

income nothing could be spared for education. But with us this was not the case, as at this time no less than five of us were at school. The schoolmaster of the village, Mr O'May, who had the evils of poverty and decrepitude to contend with, on one of his visits to the house was pleased to express a fondness for me and, stroking my white hair, enquired when I was coming to school. As the chief reason for my not going was given as my inability to pronounce the letter 'R' he soon enabled me to surmount that difficulty by allowing me to call it an 'L'. At considerably under five years of age, I was therefore sent to learn the rudiments of the English language.

The progress I made in reading greatly exceeded the expectations of both my parents. Indeed, I made a more rapid advance then than ever afterwards, and before the completion of my fifth year I could read a chapter of the Bible with tolerable exactness. When, in spring, the foundation of the building is laid, we find it best to continue our operations even though they be slow, for if the storms of winter are allowed to attack what has been done, all will soon be ruinous and dilapidated. In like manner, if the foundation of education is laid in the springtime of life it is best to be constantly added to, otherwise the businesses, curses, and anxieties of ripe years will not only prevent us from advancing, but reduce what has already been accomplished to mould and decay. But my parents, having no view of being able to advance any of us in life by means of learning, therefore carried our education no further than the competent knowledge of reading, an indifferent knowledge of writing, and a very scanty stock of arithmetic. My knowledge of the two latter branches, later being exposed to many years' disuse almost vanished, and had it not been for favourable circumstances to be narrated later, I might at this moment be unable to write my own name.

After two years working with my uncle he obtained an advantageous lease of another bleach field, and to that place we removed. Here my father continued in the capacity of boiler, while the wages of my second sister were advanced to 5s a week, while my elder sister was constantly employed embroidering muslin. I had now been a year at school and my tutor wished to put me in the writing class. My father thought then, and I think now, that I was considerably too young, but these scruples were at length overcome. Mr O'May, judging from the speed at which I had acquired my reading, imagined I would make equal progress in writing but, indeed, this is a branch of knowledge in which I never arrived at even a moderate degree of perfection, an accomplishment the want of which I have all through life often felt, and often bitterly lamented.

It is a frequent and just observation that when those who are related by ties of family also stand connected with each other by the ties of 'master' and 'servant' they seldom agree, the connection between my father and my uncle verifying the truth of this remark. My uncle possessed a good many qualities, sanguine when projecting schemes and indefatigable in following them up, though with a certain fund of haughtiness that threw a shade over them. From being much accustomed to command, and little to obey, he became to be seen by his enemies as being both arrogant and overbearing. Too frequently, however, this in an energetic spirit proves hurtful, for when the schemes were of his own invention nothing was allowed to stand in prosecution of them, and it was impossible to argue with him, while his workmen stood in fear of error. I have seen some so agitated by his presence that they were scarce able to proceed with their work, and were thus led to commit those faults they were so energetically striving to avoid. Notwithstanding this, I believe he showed much kindness to my mother on my father's death, and always showed a great deal of attention to me; so much so, that even as I write he has stood security for me to my employers to the amount of £150.

The rupture between him and my father occasioned us removing to the vicinity of Neilstone, where my father and two elder sisters immediately got employment in the bleach field of Springbank. My elder brother was engaged as a servant at a neighbouring farm, while those of the younger branches of the family, myself included, were sent to a cotton factory.

Shortly afterwards, my father decided to quit the bleaching business and remove to Paisley to take up the trade of weaving, which was at that time yielding a good income to those that followed it. Accordingly, in 1798 we moved to Paisley, leaving my two eldest sisters at Springbank.

Notwithstanding the increase of my father's income, none of us could remain at school after we were old enough to work. Accordingly, after a short probation as an assistant, on 25 March 1799 I was placed on a loom to ply the shuttle. But as my propensity was for an open, active life, this business was too close and sedentary for me. I therefore sauntered much of my time in idleness, and though often reproved and sometimes chastised, I never had the spirit of application instilled into me. My father, in order to withdraw my mind from the giddy trifles which occupied it, gave me as a task to commit to memory the multiplication tables, and though he made me sensible of having them by rote, yet such was my ineptitude to application that he never saw me master of them. Since then, however, by way of making amends to him, I have extended the table from 12x12 to 19x19.

About this time I began to acquire a pretty strong inclination for reading and, with an appetite at once voracious and unmethodical, consumed with avidity everything that came my way. This, like an appetite surcharged with food, only clogged me, and I gained little or no benefit from all I read. The thread of an interesting narrative, and an ardent desire to know the ultimate fate of the personages it concerned, hurried me on, and I paused not to reflect on the real motives that stimulated the action, to weigh the arguments adduced, or to reflect upon observations made, but like a traveller thinking only on the end of his journey, I pressed forward without observing, and consequently without enjoying the beauties which everywhere presented themselves to view. Had many others enjoyed my opportunities, their minds would have been stored with the knowledge of the characters of many of the greatest men of antiquity. They would, in short, have been in possession of a fund of general knowledge both useful and ornamental. But for want of arranging and digesting, I can recall very little when I have occasion, nor can I trace that little to the source from which it originally derived. Consequently, such facts lie as a confused collection of lumber, of little service to their proprietor. I may be compared to a person with a great quantity of stone, lime, and timber, but who cannot make himself a shelter, while many with one fourth the materials can possess themselves of a commodious dwelling. Amongst the books, however, which fell my way was the history of Robinson Crusoe. This I read over and over with avidity and delight. I rejoiced at his success, grieved at his misfortunes, and trembled when he was exposed to danger. I often wished I had been his companion, and regretted that I was not following that line of life which would put me in the way of meeting similar adventures.

I continued at the weaving business until the summer of 1803, at which time trade was exceedingly depressed and work nowhere to be found. Although fond of play, I soon became tired of total idleness, and resolved rather to get into action.

2. I leave home and join the King's service: July 1803

ON THE MORNING OF 23 July 1803, having kept my bed longer than usual, my mother being absent and no other person in the house, I borrowed from a neighbour 6d in my mother's name. With this, and the clothes in which I stood, I set out for Greenock to try my fortune at sea. Walking and running alternately, and with an occasional lift behind a carriage, I soon reached Port Glasgow. I laid out one third of my money on bread and ale, but received a penny from the driver of the car by holding his horse while he and his companion took a glass or two of whisky. So that when I reached the town from which I was to make my debut into the wide world my fortune consisted of only 5d.

Upon my arrival, I began to walk the quays in the hopes of getting a situation in some merchant vessel. But I was ill qualified as there was a kind of timidity or bashfulness attached to me, which prevented me applying to anyone, so after wandering the whole afternoon in the vain hope of being taken notice of, I was compelled as night drew on, to retire and seek a lodging. This I at last procured in a house near the shore, where I got my bed and supper, which was of Scottish sowens,[27] for 3d. After this, I retired to reflect upon the events of the day.

I had never before been absent from my father's house without the consent of my parents but had left them that morning without a single clue by which my route might be traced, and now found myself, still under fourteen years of age, further from home than I had ever been before, with a very small sum of money, and without a single friend to apply to for assistance or advice. While the persuasion of such a friend would have easily prevailed with me to go back to Paisley, a certain sense of shame prevented me doing so of my own accord. The circumstance, however, pressing heaviest on my mind was my want of success in procuring employment. And I feared it would be no better on the morrow. The 2d I had remaining could not support me more than another day, and then what was to become of me? These and many other melancholy thoughts carried across my mind in rapid succession, but at length sleep overpowered me, and suspended, for a time, all my cares and sorrows in balmy repose.

The next morning I made a few further applications for employment, as unsuccessful as they were feeble. My appearance was that of the land, and my address timid and irresolute. I would have engaged with any shipmaster for my meat and clothing, but found no one to accept any of my services on any terms. Heavy-hearted and with a dejected and long countenance, I strolled about uncertain of what to do, or whither to go. In this pensive and solitary mood, about noon I was accosted by two boys older than myself, who enquired whether I wanted a ship. This was like music to my ears, and with haste and joy I answered in the affirmative. They informed me this was also the object they had in view, and were just then repairing to a press gang rendezvous to enter the King's service, and invited me to accompany them.

Notwithstanding my forlorn condition, I could not think of yielding to their solicitations as I had often heard of the harshness of the treatment received on board war vessels, of the close confinement experienced, and of the inadequacy of the remuneration. I told them I was in search of a situation in the merchant service, where the wages were higher than in the Navy, the usage and provisions preferable, and the liberty more extensive, and where a practical knowledge of seamanship would be much sooner acquired. They, in their turn, stated that the chance of prize money in the Navy more than counterbalanced the difference of wages, that there were more hands in a King's ship and therefore the work was much easier, and that, as practical seamanship there was more neatly executed, we could all learn to a better purpose. Moreover, if we showed ourselves active and enterprising, we might meet with encouragement and promotion. These arguments would not have prevailed with me, as I was greatly prejudiced against the King's service, but as we walked along an incident occurred which determined my choice and influenced my future destiny.

One of the lads, whose name was John Shaw, found a banknote of one guinea,[28] which he immediately declared belonged equally to us all. We repaired to a tavern for some refreshments, in settling for which 2d of change was required. At this, my total remaining stock was appropriated, my remaining hope of support now being fixed on my one third share of the remainder of the guinea. I expected it would have at once been divided, but Shaw thought it proper to remain treasurer while still entertaining us with hopes of ultimate equal division. But his promises to me were never fulfilled, for while he and his companion, whose name was John Wyn, both from Glasgow, provided themselves with as many little seagoing articles as they thought necessary, I was put off with a single donation of a horn spoon. After rambling about the greater part of the day, at evening we repaired to the rendezvous. Here we found a lieutenant of the Navy to whom we offered our services, and as hostilities with France had lately commenced they were readily accepted. We then underwent a surgical examination, found ourselves to be sound in body, and less than an hour after, were on board a war vessel a mile or two from shore.

On the second day of my being aboard, my father, who had heard of me being seen on the road to Greenock, and who had rightly conjectured my route, came down to search for me. I did not know he had come on board, for when he arrived I was squatting on the deck of the press room, listening to moving accounts of battle and storm that had befallen some of the older seamen. Suddenly, the bosun's mate, with a stentorian voice, bawled down the hatchway, 'Pass the word for the boy, Robert Hay below!' At this, 'You boy, Hay! You boy, Hay!' immediately reverberated throughout the press room. I went to the hatchway to see what was wanted.

'Let me see you hand yourself up here pretty smartly', said the bosun's mate, 'or else this here switcher of mine', rattling his rattan cane on the sides of the hatchway, 'and your corduroy jacket will soon come into close quarters! And if they do', said he, turning his quid of tobacco in his cheek, and smiling at his own wit, 'I know who will come off second best.'

In the press room no ladder is allowed, the only means of ascent being a rope with knots at short distances from each other. What with hands frequently sliding up and down, and some of the wags on board bringing it in contact with the cook's grease bucket, this had become so slippery it might well have been an eel suspended in the hatchway. One of the oldest seamen, seeing my difficulties, cried out, 'On deck there! You might as well send down a rope's end with a bowline in it for this here fellow! For if he gets up that there slushy rope between this and Tib's Eve,[29] and that is neither before Christmas nor after it, there is no snakes in Virginia!' A rope's end was sent down, I was slung by the middle like a monkey, and sent dangling up the hatchway amid the jokes and laughter of the knowing ones.

On deck I found, to my great surprise, my father. At our meeting, at which both joy and grief mingled, I also observed in his paternal countenance a mixture of anger and pity, in that he had been to much expense and toil in bringing me forward thus far, and now when I might have begun to be useful to him, and of financial assistance in bringing up the younger branches of the family, I had basely deserted him. Still, he looked on me with a kind tenderness and immediately applied with urgency to the captain for my discharge. But this would not be obtained without advancing a sum of which he, alas, was not master.

'Furthermore', the captain told him, 'hands are too scarce just now as hostilities with France have just commenced, and hot as the press is, we cannot get a sufficient supply of seamen. Your son, it is true, will not be of much use for some time, but if I can judge by the cut of his jib, we have the makings of a smart fellow.' My father, therefore, was constrained to leave me, young, destitute, and inexperienced as I was, to my own fortune.

It is impossible to describe the feelings of my distressed mother once my father had set off to find me. Racked with uncertainty, with grief and bitterness of heart, she counted the hours of my father's absence, until he arrived home and announced to her the dreadful intelligence that plunged her into a flood of tears. Her grief knew no bounds. When she attempted to suspend it in sleep, the image of her favourite child, defenceless and helpless as he was in the hands of strangers, exposed to the harsh treatment and evil examples to be met with on board ship, darted across her mind, and roused her from her broken slumbers to endure the miseries of her waking thoughts.

A few days afterwards, my father, accompanied by my sister Jean, came again to visit me. He brought me some articles of clothing adapted to my new profession: a suit of true blue as a substitute for the jacket and breeches which had evoked the wit of the bosun's mate a few days before, and a fancy brab sky-scraper from the Spanish Main to circumscribe my brow instead of the chequered produce of Kilmarnock.[30] My sister furnished me with some needles, thread, and a number of little articles of which she supposed I might stand in need, together with a little bread of my mother's preparation.

They remained on board with me several hours and gave me many instructions for the regulation of my future conduct. My father charged me sedulously to avoid drunkenness and swearing, two vices very prevalent in the seafaring profession, and into which many fall when exposed to bad example. He charged me to behave to my superiors with deference, and perform the duties appointed to me with promptitude and cheerfulness, to embrace every opportunity of reading and improving myself in writing and arithmetic, to keep up constant correspondence with him, and minutely to acquaint him with all the circumstances of my prosperity, or adversity, that might befall. At parting, he gave me a Bible and charged me never to be without one. Above all, he told me as we descended the ship's side, to implore in frequent prayer constant guidance and support from that being who alone can shield you from every danger, support you under every trial, and counsel you in every emergency. My sister, bathed in tears, and deprived by grief from giving vent to her feelings, could only squeeze my hand. The boat then pushed off while my father bade me an affectionate farewell, the last words I was destined ever to hear from his lips.

We remained at Greenock about three weeks, at the end of which time sufficient hands having been collected to freight a small cutter, fifty or sixty of us, chiefly boys, were put on board one, the *Prince William Henry*, for the purpose of being conveyed to Plymouth. After being a day or so at sea, the wind veered ahead and, as it blew pretty strong and prevented us from making any progress to windward, we ran for shelter to Lamlash, Isle of Arran. It was here I first repented of having gone to sea. The vessel was small, and although the sea was smooth, she rolled and pitched considerably. I became seasick. The effluvia arising from the numerous breaths, joined to the smell of tarred rope, made it impossible for me to stay below. Indeed, the certain operation which seasickness usually produces rendered it necessary for me to remain on deck, exposed to the fury of the wind and rain, the braving of which was a lesson I had yet to learn.

The wind soon became fair and our stay here was of short continuance, but we had not proceeded far when the wind against us compelled us to run into Belfast Lough, where we anchored abreast Carrickfergus. Here we found a big tender, the *Maria*, shortly to sail to Plymouth, and as she was a larger vessel than the cutter, with a more capacious press room, the greater part of us were put on board to await a change of wind. When ascending the side of this tender, our knives were taken from us, except from one or two, last aboard, who seeing what was going forward, took the precaution of secreting theirs in some part of their clothing. One knife was allowed at every meal for each mess to divide the provisions, but had to be returned when the meal was finished. We consoled ourselves with the hope they would be restored to us when we quit the vessel, but in this we were disappointed. For when we asked for them as we were about to return to the cutter, we were only laughed at, with not even a pretext being assigned to this piece of injustice. We now had had a practical illustration of that common phrase 'to come Paddy over us'.

During the remainder of our passage we experienced no interruption except one night's anchorage in the calms of Dublin. We were now considerably more comfortable than before, as about a score of the oldest and most refractory boys were left aboard the Irish tender, those of us remaining being of a more passive disposition. But having a good deal more room, we were tolerably well accommodated.

3. *Resolu* (examination ship) and *Salvador del Mundo* (guard ship) – Plymouth: August 1803

AFTER A PASSAGE OF three weeks from Greenock we arrived at Plymouth, and were immediately sent on board the *Resolu*, a kind of examination ship appointed to receive and cleanse all new levies raised in this port. After being thoroughly washed in a number of cisterns fitted around the side of this vessel, we were then examined in a state of nudity before a committee of surgeons. Those who had any appearance of disease or uncleanliness were kept on board for cure or puri-fication. The rest, of which number I happened to be one, were sent on board the *Salvador del Mundo*, a three-deck ship taken from the Spaniards during the preceding war and which now lay as a guard ship in the harbour, a guard ship being usually an obsolete vessel permanently anchored for the reception and temporary accommodation of seamen.

From descriptions I had heard given during the passage, I had formed some idea of the appearance of a three-deck ship, but found this far short of reality. The noise and bustle upon this vessel astonished me.

On the lower deck, appropriated to the ship's crew, almost every berth was converted into a shop or warehouse where commodities of every description might be procured: groceries, haberdashery goods, hardware, stationery, everything, in fact, that could be named as the necessities or luxuries of life. Even spirituous liquors, though strictly prohibited, were to be had in abundance, the temptations of the enormous profits arising from their sale overcoming any fear of punishment. Even those who were appointed as watchmen to prevent their entrance could not withstand the alluring temptation, and were joined in this enriching trade. And while this practice was winked at where any of the crew were concerned, the most rigid scrutiny in all other cases was most carefully observed. The East India Company are not more jealous of their China tea trade than were the crew of the *Salvador* in the trade of gin and rum, and foolhardy would have been the luckless wight of a greenhorn who should attempt to disturb this profitable monopoly.

On the day I joined, a seaman's wife came to see her husband, who had been pressed a few days before. The ship's corporal, who was helping her up the accommodation ladder, took it into his head that the calves of her legs, at which he had been taking an unmannerly peep, were rather more bulky than usual.

'I am afraid, my good woman', said he, 'that your legs are somewhat dropsical; will you allow me the

honour of performing a cure?' Without waiting for
permission, he took out his knife and made a small
incision in her stocking, about a span above the heel.
The point of the knife gently pierced the skin, not of the
leg, but the bladder that that was snugly secured there:
down came a flood of liquor that made the eyes and lips
of the onlookers water, while both colour and smell bore
ample testimony that the blood of the sugar cane had
been shed. It was, in fact, a drop of sterling stingo.[31]
The poor woman, amidst blushes and apologies upon
her part, and the muttered execrations and regrets of
everyone else, but without being allowed to exchange a
single word with her husband, was immediately sent
back ashore in the boat that brought her off.

As those who were of the regular ship's crew were
but few in number, and chiefly employed manning
officers' boats, it might be thought this lower deck a
desirable berth, but as the greater number kept their
wives and families on board, it was pretty much
crowded day and night. The middle and upper decks
were set aside for the supernumeraries, the general
name for those not yet allotted to any ship.

It would be difficult to give any adequate idea of the
scenes these latter two decks presented: complexions of
every varied hue, and features of every cast, from the
jetty face, flat nose, thick lips and frizzled hair of the
African, to the more slender frame and milder features
of the Asiatic; the rosy complexion of the English

swain, and the sallow features of the sunburnt Portuguese; people of every profession and of the most contrasted manners, from the brawny ploughman to the delicate fop; the decayed author and bankrupt merchant who had eluded their creditors; the apprentices who had run from servitude; the improvident and impoverished father who had abandoned his family, and the smuggler who had escaped by flight the vengeance of the laws. Costumes ranged from the kilted Highlander, to the shirtless sons of the British prison house, to the knuckle ruffles of the haughty Spaniard, to the gaudy and tinselled trappings of the dismissed footman, to the rags and tatters of the city beggar. Here, a group of half-starved and squalid wretches, not eating, but devouring with rapacity, their whole day's provisions at a single meal; there, a gang of sharpers at cards or dice, swindling some unsuspecting booby out of his few remaining pence. To the ear came a hubbub little short of Babel: Irish, Welsh, Dutch, Portuguese, Spanish, French, Swedish, Italian, together with every provincial dialect prevailing between Land's End and John O'Groats. There was poetry being recited; failed thespians with their mutterings; songs, jests, laughter, while the occasional rattle of the boatswain's cane, and the harsh voices of his mates, blended with the shrill and penetrating sound of their whistles, served at once to strike terror into the mind, and add confusion to the scene.

The work carried on board was trifling. It consisted chiefly in hoisting aboard the provisions and water, and in keeping the ship clean. Sometimes, indeed, when another ship in the harbour was fitting out, a few ropes might be made for her, but this happened but occasionally. Notwithstanding the great number of hands on board, it was with considerable difficulty that the decks were ever washed. The seamen saw this duty beneath them while so many greenhorns and landsmen were available; while these latter, in their turn, supposed the seamen had no more right than themselves to be exempted from this duty. All hands, therefore, skulked below as much as possible. Down would come the boatswain's mates, cutting to the right and left with their switches while all fled like frightened sheep before them, but no sooner flying up one hatchway than immediately descending another, so that a constant warfare and chase was kept up.

The first sound that breaks the stillness of the night is uttered at five o'clock in the morning. It consists of a 'Whe-e-e-ugh all hands! Wash decks! A-ho-o-y!' Every eye opens while every scheme that promises extension from this irksome duty is pondered, though all remains quiet. Then, after a few moments, 'Do you hear the news there below? Come, jump up here, every mother's son of you!'

Still all is quiet. Bosun's mates are in general no way remarkable for their stock of patience, and finding no

one starting, one of them springs down, lantern swing-
ing in one hand and a rattan cane in the other, and
begins cutting away right and left. Those whose beds
are on the deck are caught at once and immediately fly
towards the hatchways like so many rats with terriers
in pursuit. The clearing of the hammocks is not so easy,
but it must be done. The mates press their shoulders
against every one of them, roaring out with voices like
thunder 'A sharp knife, a clear conscience, and out or
down is the word!' Then the hammock lanyard is cut
and, head first, down comes the occupant. Even so, it
was with difficulty this duty was enforced, and the
scrubbing brushes, holy stones, buckets, brooms and
swabs, were often not half manned.

Though these duties were in the main trifling,
everyone on the ship was anxious to leave. So when
any ship in harbour required a party of men for
sailing, all the supernumeraries were called to muster,
and each stood attentively listening in the anxious
hope of hearing his name pronounced, the names of
those destined for transfer perhaps being pitched
upon according to country, age, ability, time of having
been on board, etc., and great gladness was always
seen portrayed in the countenances of those ordered to
hold themselves in readiness to quit the ship, while
vexation and disappointment appeared equally
conspicuous in the faces of those were commanded to
go back down below.

I was witness to many of these scenes, and to as many disappointments. But at length, after having been on board several weeks, I was, with the rest of the supernumerary boys, called to muster. A Lieutenant Archibald, commander of the *Eling*, schooner, was on board to be furnished with a load of six boys for a cruise. The favour was granted to him with choosing his own six, and I, to my great satisfaction, happened to be one of them.

4. On board the *Eling* (schooner): August-December 1803

I FOUND MYSELF A great deal happier on board the *Eling* than at any time since I left home. I was often sent on various errands in the boat, frequently ashore without any officer present. This, when compared with the restrictions to which I had hitherto been exposed, was seen by me as the very essence of liberty. Besides, I had the pleasure of finding the crew a set of prime seamen, and very agreeable fellows withal. The crew of all small vessels, like other small communities, being much better known to each other and much more knitted together than the crews of large vessels, I soon became acquainted with every man on board and as I endeavoured to conduct myself towards all in as obliging a manner as possible, I soon gained their favour and their instruction.

The schooner belonged to the Guernsey station, and was sent shortly after we joined on a cruise of Grenville and Cherbourg, two ports on the coast of France, and it was before the former of these places where I saw my first shot fired in wrath. We, in company with a frigate, two bomb ships, and some smaller vessels, bombarded the town for two days with a heavy and well-directed fire that saw a great number of the inhabitants leaving, and scampering over the summit of a neighbouring hill to safety. During this time the frigate got into shallow water, the ebb tide grounding her, and laying her on her beam ends. In this condition she was quite disabled, unable to fire a gun in her own defence. The enemy, thinking this a good opportunity to attack her, sent out a number of gunboats for that purpose, but our schooner, and the other small vessels between her and the land, succeeded in beating them off. Grape and canister we gave them so hotly, that several were sunk, and the rest soon pulled back to harbour. At high water the frigate tripped her anchor and warped off into deep water without having received any injury, our antagonists being further galled by seeing us leisurely sailing about dredging for oysters, a famous bank of these lying but a few miles from the town.

During this cruise, I began to find my sea legs and got the landward appearance somewhat brushed off; I was taught to box the compass, steer in moderate weather, heave the lead, go expeditiously aloft and to be of some service once I was up. I fear my modesty did not at this time keep pace with the acquisition of my nautical knowledge. When I first went aboard the *Eling* I was reputed to be the quietest and most civil of all the boys, but before leaving I recollect hearing one of the crew observe that I was getting spoiled, and that if he mistook not, I would soon be as saucy as the rest. This remark affected me much, and made me resolved to be more affable and modest.

The cruise continued only three or four months, as the wear and tear on a vessel during a winter cruise in the Channel is very great. In that short space we found ourselves so much damaged in hull, sails, and rigging, etc., that the commodore deemed it necessary to send us to England to refit. We left St Malo about the middle of December 1803, and touching Jersey and Guernsey for dispatches and letters, arrived in two days at Plymouth.

5. I return to the *Salvador del Mundo*, and attempt to desert: December 1803

ONE FORENOON, LYING AT Stonehouse Pool, one of the creeks in Plymouth Harbour, I was greatly surprised to see a ten-oared barge from the *Salvador del Mundo*, guard ship, come alongside with an enquiry as to whether a boy by the name of Hay was on board. I was commanded to get myself and my things ready to go on board and, while rowing across, my mind was at full stretch to find out what could occasion the extra-ordinary transfer. I considered the prospect of something having been done for me – or, conversely, that I had unknowingly been guilty of some offence and that I was being summoned to receive punishment.

On board, however, my hopes and fears were at once dissipated when I learned that my father had been uneasy that I had not yet written home, and had sent a letter to the captain of the guard ship enquiring what had become of me. Captain Dilkes had politely answered the letter immediately, informing my father where I was, and promising as soon as I returned to port I would write, and it was for this purpose I had been called aboard. As I had, in great measure, forgotten my writing, the captain's clerk wrote a letter in my name and on completion I was sent back to the *Eling*. As none of the *Salvador*'s boats were going in that direction for some time, I took the opportunity of walking round her decks, witnessing those scenes from which I myself had lately escaped and which I hoped (vain hope) that I would never again be called upon to join.

Towards evening, a party of boys was appointed to one of the line-of-battle ships *(Dreadnought,* triple-decker) lying in Cawsand Bay. As the *Eling* was not far out of their way, I was put into a boat which had also been visiting the *Salvador* and the officer of this boat was ordered to put me on board the *Eling* as he passed. As the wind, however, was blowing pretty fresh from the south-west, the officer was unwilling to go so far to leeward as the *Eling*, saying he would put me aboard on his return from the *Dreadnought*. At this return, the breeze had freshened considerably, and as the night was very dark the officer again was apprehensive about going alongside the *Eling*. Instead, we went to a wet dock on the south-west side of the harbour where the officer decreed that I should sleep aboard that night, and would be put aboard the *Eling* the following morning. I awoke pretty early, and seeing a plank between the vessel and the shore, and no sentinels keeping watch, thought it an opportunity to effect an escape. And without considering my inexperience, my want of means, or the danger attending such conduct, I at once put my resolution into force to abscond.

I had not the least idea of the situation of the countryside, and consequently, no idea of the direction I took. I simply turned my back to the cutter, and walked straight forward. After a considerable distance I found myself on that eminence upon which stands Lord Edgecumb's tower. From here I saw how the harbour and the land lay, and decided that if I intended to walk home (absurd thought!) my course must be northerly, and that if I intended to go by sea it must be from a place from where I could perhaps take a passage. I therefore set out for Mutton Cove ferry. I had not one farthing of money, and I could not prevail upon the ferryman to take me over. But at length I prevailed with him when, returning empty one trip, to give me a passage for my knife, far more valuable than the money demanded for the passage.

On my arrival at the dock, I immediately commenced looking for a situation in some merchant ship. Although not so nearly as timid as when I first undertook a similar task at Greenock, I met with similar repulses, and was much dispirited. A greater bar was that I was dressed in garb easily recognisable as that belonging to a ship of war. After trying nearly all the vessels to which I could obtain access, I set out for Plymouth, where I knew there were more ships lying, hoping I might be able to work my passage in some collier to the north of England, from whence I could easily find my way to Scotland. I had to pass over Stonehouse Bridge, with a toll of one halfpenny. I had no money, and no second knife, and all my solicitations and entreaties were unavailing with the tollkeeper. However, a person who had overheard what had passed was obliging enough to point out to me a footpath which led circuitously to Plymouth.

I reached Plymouth, but here again my war garb operated against me and ensured my applications met with nothing but mortifying and discouraging repulses. In fact, a merchant captain would no more have ventured to take me aboard than he would have taken a hand spike with a broad 'aar' on it, a bolt of canvas with a waved strip of green paint, or a hawser with a rogue's yarn, various markings denoting King's service property – just as my clothing and bearing now denoted me.

As it is was now dusk, I could not find a path again and chose to try my luck once more with the toll keeper. Whether passengers pay only one way crossing Stonehouse Bridge, or whether the toll man thought it needless to renew our former altercation, I know not, but I was allowed to pass without exchanging a word.

I hastened to Mutton Cove within sight of which the *Eling* had lain – to find to my disappointment that she had shifted her station, and was nowhere to be seen. After many enquiries among the watermen, I found she had hauled higher up the harbour. I then repaired to North Corner in the hopes of seeing her, but by now all was dark. My situation at this time was by no means enviable. It was the month of November, the night was very cold, and I had not tasted a morsel during the whole day and almost nothing the previous day. I had been baffled in my attempts to get a passage to Scotland, or a berth in a merchant vessel, and now had the prospect of lying all night in the open, exposed to the inclemency of the weather.

Frequently has my guardian angel brought me into disagreeable dilemmas, but never yet has she entirely abandoned me. And so, between nine and ten in the evening, I was agreeably surprised to hear the well-known voices of some of my shipmates in the *Eling* approaching the wharf in an officer's boat. They were no less surprised to find me under such circumstances, and were eager to learn what had befallen me and what brought me there at such an unreasonable hour. I satisfied their curiosity about being unable to re-board the *Eling* from the *Salvador* in as few words as possible, taking care to conceal my real motives, for I dreaded the consequences of confessing what I had intended, and was at the same time ashamed to make known my lack of success.

When I informed them how scantily I had fared since I had left the *Eling*, with that frankness, promptitude and generosity for which our seamen are celebrated, they took me to the nearest tavern where all my wants were liberally supplied. I was seated by a rousing fire, a huge dish of beef steaks, a quartern loaf, a tankard of porter, and a half pint of gin all within arm's length of me. Their business ashore was not important, and their stay was short: a message came from the lieutenant that he would not be going back aboard that night, and so I soon found myself once more aboard the *Eling*. 'Home', says the proverb, 'is home, howe'er homely.' So I found it, for my situation now, when contrasted with the hunger, cold, and anxiety I had endured since I left her, was happiness itself.

My whole fortune at that time consisted of my bed and body clothes, and these had I had left on board the cutter bringing me back from the *Salvador del Mundo*. I dared not venture to ask about them as by this my true subsequent movements should be discovered. After a few days our commander told me that I, and some other boys, were to be returned to the *Salvador*. From here I hoped, should the cutter revisit the ship, to recover my clothes. On rejoining the *Salvador*, I applied to the captain for a boat to visit the ship to which the cutter had belonged. He promised me one at the first opportunity, but I suppose, however, he forgot, and as I had not the fortitude nor indeed would have been allowed to urge my claim with impunity, time slipped past, the vessel at length went to sea, and all my small stock was lost.

This loss affected me but not so much as my return to the *Salvador*. Against the ship I had contracted a great dislike, and when I contrasted the noise, the confusion, the harshness, and the sloth with the quietness and order which prevailed on board the *Eling* my dislike increased. I was not now, however, so much imposed upon by the sweepers and petty officers. I had learned a number of fashionable sea phrases, took care to let it be known I had been in the seagoing vessel, and that I had seen service off France. Consequently, I now considered myself a step or two above the greenhorn. As is frequently done by wiser heads, I rated my abilities far too high. I knew a little, but my pride magnified that little into a great deal to verify the truth of that well-known observation that, the less know-ledge we possess the more apt we are to be puffed up with it, an attitude that exposes us to both the con-tempt and ridicule of our superiors in knowledge, and to the hatred and calumny of those over whom we ourselves haughtily assume superiority.

After remaining on board about a month, a period that seemed more like a year, I had one day the pleasure of hearing my name called, and orders were given me to get my things in readiness to prepare to quit the ship. As I had nothing but the clothing in which I stood, I was, of course, ready immediately; a little before midnight, on 31 December 1803, I found myself on board HMS *Culloden* (74 guns) lying in Cawsand Bay.

6. HMS *Culloden*: from 31 December 1803

THE DIFFERENCE BETWEEN A small schooner like the *Eling*, and a line-of-battle ship is very great. Though I could show myself tolerably active on board the former, on board the latter I was almost as ignorant as if I had left my father's fireside the day before.

Boys of the age I was then (fourteen years) seldom had any share of seaman's duties to perform on a large ship, being generally taken on as servants to the officers. So it was on the *Culloden*. On the second day we were all called onto the quarterdeck, wherein account was taken of our ages, education, time at sea, and several other particulars. An account was also made of our stock of clothing, but there were not as many articles among the eight of us as would have made one decent suit. After these accounts of ourselves and property, the officers of rank, by seniority, were each allowed to choose one of us for a servant. In this way six of us were thus disposed, while the other two, who were older and stouter, were stationed in the mizzen-top.

I was chosen by a Lieutenant Hawkins, who retained

me in his service until he quit of the ship in June 1804. This arrangement was not at all agreeable to me at first. With all my fancied skill in seamanship, to be degraded into a shoe-boy! However, my ambition was not stifled, but merely directed into another channel. For it was now my object to see that no other officer surpassed my master in a well-brushed coat, in the brilliancy of his boots and shoes, and in the neatness and order of his cabin. I was also expected to appear (which his kindness enabled me to do) clean and tidy at the back of his chair at dinner, and to take care that if he missed his share of the good things going at the wardroom table, it should be no fault of mine.

Among the books and furniture in my master's cabin were a nautical almanac, a copy of Hamilton Moore,[32] a Gunter's scale,[33] a case of mathematical instruments, a Hadley's quadrant and an excellent chart of the Channel, with the adjacent coasts of England and France. With what ecstasy did I survey these deeply interesting articles! If ever I broke the tenth commandment, and coveted my neighbour's goods, it was because of these treasures, and my master's skill in using them. By his generosity I had free access to them, and soon began to perceive how easily a knowledge of trigonometry might be converted into our knowledge of navigation. But then, how was the knowledge of the use of the quadrant in taking the sun's meridian altitude to be gained? The appearance of a servant boy

on the deck of a warship with the quadrant in his hand
would have been seen as such a flagrant breach of
discipline that five dozen over the gun would scarcely
have been atonement. But to an agile mind many
expedients will occur. A lighted candle placed on the
dressing table, elevated or depressed as circumstances
required, was made to represent the sun, and on my
knees before this minor luminary, I endeavoured to find
how to navigate. One night I had placed the candle
rather too high, and my attention being wholly taken
up in my calculations, I forgot that the rays of my
pretend sun were coming in contact with the white
painted ceiling, and by the time I had finished my
observations, there was a sooty circle three feet in
diameter, as black as coal itself. Everything was stowed
away in an instant, soap and water and towels were
procured to efface this mark, and I set to work as
vigorously as possible to exterminate these memorials.

7. Admiral Lord Collingwood:
6 February-7 May 1804

THE STATION OF THE *Culloden* at this time was that of
the British Channel, our fleet there proving a great
annoyance to our enemies, the French, in almost
annihilating their coasting trade, while scarcely a
foreign vessel could enter or leave their ports. It was on
this station that the *Culloden* had the honour to hoist
the flag of Lord Collingwood. A better seaman, a better
friend to seamen, never trod a quarterdeck. He and his
favourite dog, Bounce, were well known to every
member of the crew. How attentive he was to the health
and comfort and happiness of his crew! A man who
could not be happy under him, could be happy
nowhere, while a look of displeasure from him was as
bad as a dozen at the gangway from another man.

He took especial care of the boys. Blow high, or blow
low, he had us arranged in line on the poop every
morning, when he himself would inspect us to see we
were all clean and our clothing in good trim. We were
divided by him into three divisions – fore, main, and
mizzen – and, after each muster, each party had to race
up to the weather rigging of their respective masts to

the cross trees, then down to leeward arranging themselves on the poop in order of arrival. The fastest, of course, got furthest aft, and happy was he who made the point of honour at the stern taffrail, an honour always enjoyed either by Dennis O'Flanagan or myself. We both belonged to the foremast party, and were pretty good friends – excepting this daily race in which subsisted between us a most intense degree of rivalry.

On one certain day, Dennis had been the victor twice in succession, and now strained every nerve to gain triple victory. I was no less intense in my efforts to avoid so shameful a defeat. After inspection, the words 'Away aloft!' had scarcely left the lips of the master-at-arms when Dennis and I found ourselves alongside each other in the fore rigging. Up we went side by side, the ratlines scarcely bending beneath our tread. I passed abaft the mast, Dennis before it, and down we went still together. When within a fathom or two of the dead eyes, a ratline gave way with me, and I was thrown into the top. I was stunned for a moment. As I recovered, the first words I heard were being roared out by Dan O'Keeff, 'Well done, Dennis! By the powers you have it now! Show that bargue-eating cabogue of a Scotchman you are the boy to take the conceit out of him! Hurrah! Ireland's eyes forever!'

'Sef us, Robert, d'ye hear what that garse, kaming Erishman is saying,' exclaimed Saunders McIntosh. 'Ye'll surely no let the laurels be torn frae the brows of auld Scotland by any potato-eater that ever left the bogs! Oh man! Think of all Auld Reekie, and make all the sail you can!'

This pathetic appeal to patriotism and national honour was irresistible. The honour of Scotland seemed now to lie solely upon my shoulders. But Dennis was descending with such rapidity as left all idea of coming up with him, or rather down with him, hopeless. In this dilemma, I seized one of the backstays, and descended into the hammock netting with all the velocity that gravity itself could impart. One jump then brought me to the gangway, along which I sprang with all the agility I could muster, to reach the post of honour about six feet ahead of Dennis. The admiral, as usual, had his eye on us, and considering that I had taken unfair disadvantage of Dennis, took him by the arm and, to the unspeakable mortification of Saunders McIntosh, placed Dennis in the post of honour. But this was not all. After muster was over, he ordered me to the masthead by way of punishment.

'Defeat', said he, 'would have been no disgrace today, seeing you could have pleaded the giving way of the ratline, but it is always dishonourable to take unfair advantage of a competitor.'

While up on the masthead, I began to think of the one case in which Dennis still had advantage of me. He had sat on the highest point of the ship, the truck of the mast, a feat to which I had often aspired, and as all were now aware of my presence, I thought it was a good time to show them that I would not be outdone in this particular matter. Leaving the cross trees, and taking a turn with the signal halyards round each leg, to keep myself steady, I landed myself fairly on the truck. I took off my hat and waved it around my head. The admiral, seeing all hands staring aloft, saw me in this act.

'Main top, there, sir! Bring that boy down instantly!'

'Aye, aye, sir!' said Tom Lennox. 'Come down here my fine little fellow! My eyes, but you are sure to catch it now! Two dozen, I'll warrant, will be the least of it!' Down I came with a palpitating heart. The galley, the breech of the gun, the master-at-arms, the spun yarn seizings, and last but not least the cut of the cat-o'-nine-tails: all this passed in the view before my mind's eye. On reaching the quarterdeck, I stood trembling, hat in hand, until the admiral came forward.

'How high did I order you to go, boy?'

'To the cross trees, sir.'

'What business then had you, at the royal masthead?'

'Dennis was once up there, sir, and often taunts me about it and I thought it as good a time to show I could go there as easily as himself.' He paused for about half a minute, a partial frown clouding his features, and I thought he was considering how many dozen he would order me, but his countenance then softened, indicating that the squall I dreaded was blown over.

'Well', said he, 'I commend you for endeavouring not to be outstripped in activity when duty calls; I love to see a man striving to the point of honour in danger, but can never approve of anyone throwing his life in jeopardy for the sake of a vain boast. You may go below.'

A further way the admiral had for our improvement was to give each boy in charge to the best seamen of the mess to which he belonged, for the teaching of good behaviour and seamanship, and it was my lot to fall to John Gillies, a handier fellow than whom never left the Emerald Isle.

'Let us have the necessaries first, Robert', said he, 'and we will attend to the other matters afterwards.' Accordingly, the cutting out and making of jackets, shirts, and trousers, the washing of them when soiled, and mending of them neatly, took precedence. Then came the making of straw hats and canvas pumps. Then followed various operations in seamanship, as opportunities occurred for displaying them, or according to the importance they bore in Jack's sight. Jack had been at sea since the height of a marlin spike, and a better practical sailor was not to be found from stem to stern. From the knotting of ropes to the steering of a ship under bare poles in a typhoon, Jack excelled in all. Nor could any surpass him in the handling of a thirty-two pounder, and he could hit the mark with it as well as any fellow that ever took a match, or the lanyard of a lock, in hand. He was an excellent sailmaker, too, and there was not one piece of canvas, from the windsail to the spanker, but what he could shape and make.

He had in his youth been taken by a privateer and was two years in a French prison. There he had learned many ingenious things, from the making of a bone three-decker, with all her sails and rigging, to the tattooing of a mermaid on his arm, or that of a messmate, to the carving of a dolphin on the handle of a knife – also to play the German flute, and to talk French with a tolerable degree of volubility. All these acquisitions were at my service, and if I did not hoist them aboard the fault lay, not with Jack, but with myself. As well, he could play at least a dozen games of cards, and at fox and goose, at chequers, and at backgammon. But as he knew well that the admiral's anticipated examination would not touch upon these latter topics, we agreed to postpone them *sine die*. What may seem strange was that Jack did not know the alphabet!

'I have frequently begun', said he, 'with that fellow at the stem head', meaning the letter 'A', 'but could never get so far as that crooked gentleman', the letter 'Z', 'that is at the helm.' I cheerfully volunteered to help, but he would never muster up courage to make a determined effort.

'I have reached the latitude of two score and ten',

said he, 'and Greenwich, you know, is only a degree and a half more – which I think I will reach without any of their assistance.' In this, Jack was claiming to be fifty, and would hope to obtain admission to Greenwich Hospital for retired seamen when he became sixty-five.

But there were many other ways to show my gratitude to Jack. When it was his turn to be cook of the mess, I became his mate and would make the duff, attend to the sea pie or lob-scouse,[34] bring down the pea soup and grog, wash the traps, and make all snug. Last but not least, I would relinquish my grog in his favour. I had, indeed, as a boy, only half allowance, but my half, and his whole, made what he called 'a decent taut'. I had not yet begun to drink grog dinner and supper, and was in no great hurry to learn, as I knew this was a knowledge I could acquire at any time. And so, while my grog was the most acceptable offering I could possibly make to Jack, it was one I could do without any great sacrifices.

Jack was a very warm-hearted fellow, and I must not omit to mention an instance of his kindness. Ashore one day, in his rambles he fell in with a stand of second-hand books and, knowing my love of these articles, thought no less than to buy me one, and soon the largest and handsomest was buttoned under his jacket. I will never forget his look as he handed me the fine large quarto, bound in rough calf, and titled with gilt letters on a red leather ground. I went directly to this title page to see *Contingent Remainders*. A dry law book, nearly as closely sealed to me as to Jack himself. I would, in fact, sooner have gone to the masthead in a gale of wind than read a page of it. Seeing my features as I glanced over the table of contents, Jack's joy was greatly dampened.

'I am thinking, Robert', said he, 'I have been unfortunate in pitching on a favourite hooker for you. All I know is that she was of the largest tonnage, and the best rigged in a fleet of about two hundred, but I had not the skill to open her hatches and examine the cargo.'

Jack's principal failing, though he would never admit it, was an ardent love for a 'dhrop of the cratur'. He would have gone through fire and water for it, swimming the Hellespont for a half-gallon bladder as cheerfully as Leander ever did to visit his mistress. Eventually, it proved to him, as it always will do to its devotees, his ultimate ruin. An old shipmate and countryman came to see him one day while we lay in Hamoaze. After chatting over the delights of the Emerald Isle, the potency of her poteen, the virtue and valour of her sons, and the beauty and kindness of her daughters, Jack's friend had to be lowered down the ship's side on the end of a rope. Jack himself was found next morning, lying in the fore cockpit, his neck broken, and his body stiff and cold. The same day he was put into a coffin, landed at North Corner, and carried on the shoulders of his messmates to his long home in the vicinity of Stoke Church. After profiting by his instruction, and enjoying his unbounded confidence and unshaken friendship for six years, I now had the melancholy consolation of closing his eyes.

But to return to the admiral and his kindness. He was walking the quarterdeck one very cold day, when a main-top man, with a jacket through which the wind had free ingress, mounted the Jacob's ladder.

'Where are you going, my lad?' asked the Admiral

'Look out at the masthead, your honour.'

'Have you no warmer jacket than that to put on?'

'No other, your honour, but my mustering one.'

'Davies,' said the Admiral to his coxswain. 'How many jackets have you, Davies?'

'Four, sir.'

'Jump down and bring the second-best one here, and if you have a spare leg of a pair of trousers lying by, put it in one of the pockets.' Davies' second-best jacket, and a good one it was, soon covered the shoulders of the main-top man.

'Remind me of this Davies, the first time we go ashore.' But there was no necessity, and I scarcely need add that Davies was not a jacket out of pocket by the transaction.

Some sea officers, whose greatest fear is the fear of too much familiarity with the seamen, make a point of never addressing a man by name when they speak to him, but always by the contemptuous expression, 'You, sir!' We had one lieutenant aboard who used these words so often, he was better known as 'Mr You Sir!' than by his own name. Collingwood, who had noticed this behaviour, one day took a delicate way of hinting his dislike. This lieutenant had charge of the watch, and had been 'You sir-ing' away until the admiral lost all patience. Going aft, to where the lieutenant stood near the break of the poop, he addressed himself to the steersman, but loud enough to be heard by the lieutenant.

'Jenkins, what is that man's name in the weather-rigging?'

'Dan Swain, your honour.' Forward the Admiral went, and putting his hand, instead of the speaking trumpet, to his lips called out, 'Dan Swain!'

'Sir?'

'The after end of that last ratline is too high; let it down a hand's breath.'

'Aye, aye, sir!' The lieutenant knew right well for whom this hint was intended and forthwith expunged 'You, sir!' from his vocabulary.

Collingwood, in short, will perhaps stand second to none that ever hoisted a flag. He was as careful of the ship and her stores as if he had been sole owner. Scarcely could she be put about at any hour of the day or night, than he would be out on deck, accompanied by Bounce. When the ship was round, and the rigging taut, he would exchange a few kindly words of the lieutenant of the watch, then retire to his cot. Duties of every kind were carried with the directing hands of a master spirit. No swearing, no threatening nor bullying, nor canes to be seen, nor do I recollect a single instance of a man being flogged while Collingwood was aboard. Was discipline neglected then? By no means. There was not a better disciplined crew in the fleet, nor a ship which could manoeuvre with greater celerity. Cleanliness, for him, was a cardinal virtue, but he disdained to carry it to that finical extent which leads some commanders to polish the shot in the coamings around hatchways, or to stop the grog of a mess, because the hoops on the kid[35] that went for it did not shine with sufficient brilliancy.

And how kind was he to the sick and wounded! It would have done your heart good, as it has often done mine, to see a roasted chicken, a basin of fresh soup, a tumbler of wine or jug of negus,[36] or some other cordial, wending its way from his table to some poor fellow riding quarantine in the sick bay. And while we have men such as him, we will bid defiance to foreign intrigues and domination, and if voluptuousness and effeminacy, extravagance, neglect, and want of public spirit at home do not paralyse our efforts, then will our meteor flag wave protection to commerce, flap defiance to aggressors, flutter in the sunshine of prosperity, and brave both breeze and battle for a thousand years more.

8. Rear Admiral Sir Edward Pellew – voyage to the East Indies: July-November 1804

OUR SHIP, AFTER CRUISING the Channel four or five months, repaired to Plymouth and then to Portsmouth. There she refitted, took aboard six months' provisions, and hoisted the flag of Rear Admiral Sir Edward Pellew, lately appointed to the command of the British naval forces in the East Indies. As we were nearly refitted by the time he joined, at six o'clock in the morning of 10 July 1804, the order went forth :

'All hands up anchor, ahoy! Ship the capstan bars there, carpenters, bring to forward, jump down the tier, man, and coil away the cable.'

'Aye, aye, sir.'

'Are you ready there forward?'

'All ready, sir.'

'Heave away. What kind of a drawling tune is that, fifer? Strike up 'Off She Goes' or 'Drops of Brandy'. Keep step there, all of you, and stamp and go. Light round the messenger there, aft, hand forward the nippers, you boys.'

'The anchor is a-peak, sir.'

'Very well. Thick and dry for weighing there below.'

'Already with the topsails, sir.'

'Let fall sheet home, hoist away, brace sharp up there forward. Is the foretack down, boatswain?'

'Choke a block, sir.'

'Then haul aft, take a good pull of the bowlings, there, forward.'

'The cat is hooked, sir.'

'Clap on the cat fall there in the waist, and hoist away. We will not mind the fish, boatswain, till we are round the point.'

'Very well, sir.'

'Will she weather the point on this tack, pilot?'

'It will be touch and go, sir.'

'Then luff, boy, luff and touch her.'

'Luff it is, sir.'

'All clear for going about forward?'

'She is fairly round the point, sir.'

'Oh, very well, port a little, p-o-o-o-rt. Let go the tacks and bowlings there forward.'

'All gone, sir.'

'Ease off the sheets and lee braces there to leeward. Round the weather braces, you afterguard. How is her head, quartermaster?'

'South-west by west, sir.'

'Steady then, so steady.' And away we went down the channel with a large fleet in charge, bound for India.

As Lieutenant Hawkins was not fond of India, at his own request he was transferred to a ship on the home station. So, as soon as we cleared, I made application to the first lieutenant to be put into the mizzen-top.

'There are a number of officers, my lad', said he, 'have come aboard with the admiral and are not yet furnished with boys, but if there are enough without you to serve them, you shall have your wish.' But my wish was not to be granted. Although St Matthew tells us that no man can serve two masters, in my case one was a divine and the other a layman. Mr Dunsterville was a clergyman of the Church of England and chaplain to the ship. Mr Crease held the rank of master's mate, and had come aboard under the admiral's patronage to go to India to meet preferment.

Mr Dunsterville was of small stature, with a plump round face, and eyes peculiarly large, but not expressive. His hair was bushy and black as a raven, and his complexion dark. He was somewhat cold, stiff, reserved and formal in his manners. Towards inferiors he cultivated a propelling aspect no way calculated to gain esteem or confidence. In all his transactions, which were indeed very few, with any of the seamen, he was quite upright and faithfully observed his promises, but he was exceedingly hard withal. He was, therefore, unpopular with the crew, who generally estimate a man's goodness by his liberality. Seamen, moreover, look with a very jealous eye on anyone who enjoys too easy a berth on board, and this was considered so in his case, as it was understood he did nothing at all. The Church of England appears to require less talent and application in its ministers, particularly those appointed to naval service, than that of Scotch Presbyterians. Mr Dunsterville, besides reading prayers on a Sunday, would, when the weather permitted, deliver a sermon. But he was never under the necessity of composing any, for he brought aboard two to three dozen, more than sufficient for the whole passage. When in company with the admiral, with whom he messed, or with the lieutenants, he was quite jovial and free. He could drink a good glass, take, but rather give, a good joke, and upon the whole, among his equals, was deemed a facetious very good companion.

My second master, Mr Crease, was about five foot five or six inches high, somewhat spare in form and features, dark complexion, black sparkling eyes which penetrated like lances and which, when animated with passion, struck terror and dismay into any unfortunate enough to incur his resentment, and over whom he possessed control. In his motion he possessed all the whiffling activity of a Frenchman. His orders were delivered with such rapidity as to be frequently misunderstood, but when understood and executed with precision, he seemed to enjoy great pleasure. On the whole, he was a useful and expert officer. But he was hasty in his temper, haughty in demeanour, and arrogant and overbearing in disposition. His resentment was easily incurred, and what made it more formidable, its duration was generally coterminous with his power of displaying it.

On my first introduction to him, he spoke to me with the greatest kindness and condescension. Finding on enquiry that my stock of clothing was small, he promised to increase it and also to procure me what other little necessities I might stand in need of on so long a voyage. He also promised the use of his books, together with pen and paper, that I might improve myself in writing. I was highly gratified with such promises, resolving to avail myself of such valuable opportunities. But they turned out to be as false as they were fair. As for Mr Dunsterville, the chaplain, he made me no promises whatsoever, so in receiving nothing from him, I met with no disappointment. In the service of two such masters, it could not be expected that I could enjoy a great deal of happiness. But in what situation in this present life is any great deal of happiness to be found?

After being at sea about a fortnight, we reached the island of Madeira, anchoring at the principal port, Funchal, on 24 July 1804. The appearance of everything here was new and strange. The boats which came alongside were different from any I had seen before, the people in them more than half naked, and the greater part of the food, and other things they brought for sale, while not unknown in England, were both scarce and dear there, if found at all. Grapes, figs, dates, melons, oranges and pumpkins: all came off in great abundance and at quite a moderate price. Onions were of a very large size, and of a much milder nature than those found in England. At Funchal, we took on the supply of fresh provisions and refilled our water casks, as it was not intended we should now call at any other replenishing place until we reached India. The admiral took on board here several pipes of wine, not only for himself, but also for friends in England, wine being much more highly prized when taken to India and back, than when brought direct from Madeira.

On the same day we made the island two men fell overboard, one an expert swimmer. Although every exertion was used, we succeeded in saving neither.

After leaving Madeira, we fairly entered the trade winds; every reef was shaken out, and with the wind four points abaft the beam and constantly steady, there was no need to start tack nor sheet for several weeks. Up went the signal for the fleet to crowd all sail, and answering pennants fluttered at every royal masthead. The *Culloden* was so fast that no ship in the fleet could get more than a glance of our stern cabin windows, certainly none could see the countenance of the Duke of Cumberland, hero of Culloden field, as he stood forward on the lookout, with his back to the gammoning of the bowsprit.

Nothing happened during our voyage above the usual occurrences, although everything was new and singular to me. Immense shoals of flying fish, the existence of which youthful prejudices had led me to doubt, were seen winging their way a yard or two above the surface of the water. Chased from their native element by their enemies, the dolphins, they seek shelter in the air, but there, alas, they are doomed to meet another enemy equally rapacious, as they frequently fall during their flight into the jaws of the albatross. Even so, only once did one fly aboard the ship. It flew into one of the gun ports and was about the size, and not unlike the appearance of, a small herring.

We did, however, catch a number of dolphins on our passage. These fish seem fond of swimming a few yards ahead of the ship, probably in readiness to seize on other fish which the ship's motion disturbs. They are usually caught with a hook baited in imitation of a flying fish, and are sometimes struck with a pair of grains (an instrument consisting of six or eight barbed prongs attached to a long pole), which is thrown at them in the same manner as harpoons are thrown at whales. With the exception of their rather blunt heads, they are very pretty fish: their colours, which they frequently change after they are caught, are very splendid. Though always well relished by seamen, they are far from possessing either tenderness or an agreeable taste.

We likewise succeeded in catching a considerable number of sharks by the following method. A large hook is provided about half an inch in diameter. This is fixed to a foot or two of chain to prevent the hook from being bitten off, and to a swivel to prevent the untwisting of the rope. Pork is the bait usually taken. When the shark approaches, the hook is thrown over, and rarely does the fish refuse to bite. The mouth being placed several inches behind the point of the upper jaw causes it to turn belly up when the bait is being taken. The fish is then played with till it becomes exhausted, when it is brought to the surface. The rope attached to the hook being too weak to bring the shark aboard, a running knot is made and passed over the shark's head and tightened close to its dorsal fin. A number of men then get hold of the rope and sometimes find it necessary to apply a tackle before being able to hoist the monster on board.

At the dissection, the proprietor of the hook gets the first cut, which he always takes from the tail as the most tender part and, after he is served, the word is 'cut who can', and in a few minutes every inch of room in both the fireplace and the oven is put into requisition for the reception of pieces of the monster. The backbone is generally taken by someone for a walking cane, and the jawbone sometimes preserved as a curiosity. Between the upper and lower jaw of the one we caught, though it was only eleven feet long, I could trust my head and shoulders. From this, some idea may be formed of the jaws of those of twenty to thirty feet long. On opening one we caught one afternoon, we found the skin and meat of a sheep we had thrown overboard that morning. In another we found an eight pound piece of pork, lately snatched from another ship in the fleet. As digestion of this did not seem to have commenced, this extracted pork was taken by one of the seamen and cut into thin slices, alternated with layers of the shark itself, both being placed in a tin dish that was then put into the oven and made, according to the sailor's own account, an excellent meal.

I was somewhat surprised to see this, as shark is known to be of a very rank nature, and well-known itself to eat human flesh. On making my scruples known, he only laughed and said that had he got hold of one of us, he would soon have snapped us up, so for us to feast on him was only tit for tat. It is said of sharks, that when any danger besets their young, they swallow them to keep them out of harm's way. Certainly, in the intestines of one we caught, we found three or four living ones about a foot long. From this, we naturally concluded them have been very recently swallowed, but whether for protection or digestion we knew not. On another occasion, a little tailor was busy cutting slices from the shark's tail, but being unable to stand his ground with some stronger competitors, he was forced beneath the jaws of the shark, which by way of retaliating bit a piece out of the tailor's posterior rendering him unable to work for several weeks. On several sharks we caught we found some of their remora, or sucking fish, attached. Whether these were palatable, or unpalatable, I cannot say, for they were but small and we could not be troubled, leaving them as we had so much larger stuff to work on.

As the Cape of Good Hope was at this time in the hands of the Dutch, with whom we were at logger-heads, we gave it a wide berth, going as far south as the islands of St Paul's and Amsterdam. On the former we saw a flag shaking in the breeze. The ship was immediately hove-to, and a relief boat sent ashore with beef, pork, biscuits, spirits. On landing, we found the crew of an American schooner which had been wrecked there some time before. The crew had saved some of their provisions, and as the island produced plenty of vegetables and fresh water, and the coast abounded with fish, they lived pretty comfortably. Had we been bound for America or Europe, they would have gratefully embraced the passage, but considering the East Indies out of their way they preferred waiting on the opportunity of some vessel bound in the direction they favoured. One seaman, however, not on very good terms with his captain, joined us. His name was Robert Cruse which, given the similarity of his circumstances, we immediately converted to Robinson Crusoe.

By this time my lay master, Mr Crease, had begun to

use me with a degree of severity and harshness I thought unmerited. This, joined to the failure of all his first promises, now alienated my affections, so that it is probable my services wanted that respect which should have accompanied them. He became harsh and tyrannical; I became discontented and sullen. From threats he proceeded to blows, and not infrequently used a rope's end across my shoulders. The breach becoming daily wider, at length one evening I lodged a complaint with Captain Cole, a friend of Admiral Pellew. Cole, although a strict disciplinarian, was neither oppressive himself, nor would he tolerate oppression in others. Finding on enquiry that my complaints were well founded, Mr Crease was immediately sent for, and in the presence of a number of offices and seamen was severely reprimanded. He was relieved of my services, and told that as he did not seem to know how to treat a boy, he should not have another while he remained in the ship.

It may easily be supposed what effect such a reprimand had with a man of Mr Crease's temper. His countenance became pale, and his lips quivered with rage. His eyes darted fury and his teeth chaffed together like a wild boar. Had I been at his mercy, I verily believe he would have ground me to powder in a twinkling. The knowledge that he had no longer the liberty to chastise me only increased his rage and hatred, and he became from that time the most implacable enemy I ever had the misfortune of encountering.

After this, my services were confined to Mr Dunsterville alone and as I had a good deal of spare time, and realising that time is wealth, I took care to waste as little as possible. Besides the numerous items of knowledge Jack Gillies was ever ready and willing to communicate, I desired to learn the art of keeping the account of the ship's way. I had for this purpose procured a second-hand chart of the world, on Mercator's projection, and this, small and imperfect as it was, proved very useful. To get any opportunity of taking the meridian altitude of the sun, and thereby ascertaining latitude, was, of course, wholly out of the question. But circumstances occurred which enabled me to get the ship's place almost every day and then to trace on the chart with a pencil her daily progress. It was a rule aboard that every midshipman should send in daily to the captain, on a slip of paper, a statement of the course and distance made since the day previous, together with the bearings and distance of the point of land we intended first to make. These slips, quaintly called 'the day's works', were generally handed to the wardroom sentinel, who sent them into the captain by one of the boys. I took care to throw myself frequently in the way of these little errands, and had thus the means of seeing, almost every day, the ship's place at noon.

Our passage to India was on the whole very pleasant. The admiral and Captain Cole both knew the advantages of cheerfulness in a ship's company, and embraced all opportunities of bringing it into play. In the evenings, the instrument of Black Bob the fiddler was in almost constant requisition, giving spirit to the evolutions of those who were disposed to trip it a little on the light fantastic toe. Invigorating and enlivening games went on in all quarters, and if there happened to be more dancers than could get conveniently within the sound of Bob's fiddle, the admiral's band was ordered up.

This band, however, was a means of placing us once in considerable jeopardy. One of the ships in the fleet had a good many ladies aboard and the captain, being a man of gallantry, as all good seamen are, sometimes ran his vessel under our quarter to regale his passengers with proceedings from our poop. One afternoon, having shaved us rather close, our spanker took the wind out of his head sails, and before we knew what we were about his spritsail yard was locked in our main rigging. What alarmed us most, our lower deck ports were all up, and if she had heeled much she would have given the water free passage through them, and it is hard to say what might have been the result. However, the ports were all closed and secured with the utmost expedition, and then all our attention was directed to get the Indiaman boomed off. This we succeeded in doing, but not until she had sprung her spritsail yard, carried away a piece of her cat head, and started her bumpkin from its seat. All her captain's gallantry, thenceforth, could not overcome his antipathy toward music. It all became as a discord to his ears, and he took care, ever after, to give us a wide berth.

9. Arrival in the East Indies –
Pulopenang, Bombay, Madras:
November 1804-May 1805

WHEN OUR FLEET HAD fairly entered the Bay of Bengal we parted company. The Indiamen went straight to the north for Bengal, while we shaped our course to the eastward for Prince of Wales Island, where we arrived on 27 November 1804, our passage having been twenty weeks. We expected there Admiral Ranier, whom Sir Edward was to succeed in command, but learned that he had shortly before sailed for Madras. There we followed him, but heard on our arrival that he, in turn, had now gone to Pulopenang to meet us. Our arrival at Madras Bay happened during the stormy season, called the monsoon, a time when no ships consider it safe, nor are permitted to anchor. Our stay here was short as we soon returned to Pulopenang, where Admiral Ranier joined us and delivered up to Sir Edward the command of all the naval forces in India.

Mr Dunsterville, my master, often went ashore in this port and on some occasions took me with him. Notwithstanding his keeping me very short of pocket money, I was exceedingly fond of these occasions. He

was a frequent visitor at the house of the governor, and
while he was being regaled inside, I had liberty to
roam about the gardens. All the trees, bushes, shrubs
and flowers were new to me, and I was never tired
gazing on them, while coconuts, watermelons, mangoes, oranges, lemons, limes, plantains, bananas,
cashew nuts, chillies, etc., grew in the greatest abundance. Initially, an orange tree attracted my particular
attention. Much larger than the common size, it was
decked with the most beautiful foliage of leaves and
blossoms, while green and yellow fruit blended their
various hues and greatly enhanced its beauty. As it was
about noon, with the sun at its most intense, the
orange tree held out the gracious prospect of sheltering
me from the heat, while allaying my thirst by its
produce. I ascended it, resolving to repose myself
among its shady branches and feast on its delicacies,
when suddenly I found all the naked parts of my body
completely covered with pismires which attacked me
incessantly with tormenting stings.[37] My efforts to
shake them off proving ineffectual, I dropped
precipitately from the tree, and by rolling in the sand
and plunging into the water was soon quit of my
tormentors, but their effects continued many days
after. Thus it is that moments of pleasure are
frequently followed by hours, days, and weeks of pain.
Thus I learned, though doubtless often forgot it again,
that before yielding to voluptuous enjoyment, we

should estimate with as much care and precision as possible the probable consequences.

The poorer classes of people at this and most of the other ports in India wear very little covering on their bodies. A piece of cord is tied around their middle to which one end of a narrow piece of cloth, a yard or two long, is affixed. The other end, after being passed between their legs, is tucked carelessly around the waist cord. Those in easier circumstances wind several yards of cotton cloth around their middles and sometimes take a turn of it over the shoulders. Those in high life generally wear a loose robe which covers the arms, the body, and halfway down the legs. Stockings are never worn, and the feet of those a degree or two removed from poverty are covered with slippers of coloured leather, or with sandals. All are partial to rings, not only in the ears and on the fingers, but often on the toes with sometimes a large one suspended from the middle membrane of the nose. In addition, the female sex usually wear rings or bracelets around the wrists and ankles, and generally have one fold of their loose garment brought over their heads.

The head of the male sex, unless the owner is very poor indeed, is much better attended to than the body. Their headdress, called a turban, consists of a piece of narrow muslin, usually white, but sometimes varie-gated with red and blue. It can be from three or four yards long to thirty or forty, according to the fancy and funds of the wearer. It is passed round the head, turn by turn, with great exactness and care, and frequently extends to a circle large enough to shelter the shoulders from the sun's vertical rays. On the top, the folds are so disposed as to form a convenient receptacle for a few leaves of a peculiar kind, together with some chunam, and beetle nut, all of which they passionately blend together and chew as seamen do tobacco.

The natives of this place, and nearly the whole of the East Indies, are very different in appearance from the coast of Guinea Negroes. In general, they are not quite so black, and of a much more regular and handsome shape. Their features are pleasing, their hair long and smooth, and, colour excepted, they come pretty near the European idea of beauty. They are much more distinguished for effeminacy, pusillanimity and sloth, than for hardihood, bravery or diligence. They cannot, on the whole, be termed of a vindictive spirit, yet there are some instances where Europeans engaging in a trade usually followed by the natives have been poisoned. They do not seem very ingenious; at least I have observed that watchmaking and other professions where ingenuity is required being mostly in the hands of the Chinese, a great many of whom are settled at this port. They are much more strict in their religion than in their morals, and many who would refuse to drink from the same vessel as a European, would not scruple to cheat him of a rupee. They may be said to be pretty much addicted to thieving, and when detected are often made to work in chains at the direction and repair of public works, or driving piles for a new wharf.

We are often led by our prejudices to censure in others practices from which we ourselves are far from being exempt. We blame these people with being addicted to knavery, but certain it is they receive frequent lessons in this art from British seamen. I will mention an example or two. It was a standing rule that no seamen were permitted to exchange articles of clothing for any of the commodities that came alongside for sale, which meant that when bartering took place it was all performed in an underhanded way, and thus none of the articles of barter could be examined in detail. One of our crew had a red flannel shirt, an article to which the natives are very partial. Resolving to make the most of it, he cut it into four pieces – back, front and two sleeves. He enclosed in each of these pieces as much rubbish to make the size of a full shirt, and sold each piece into different boats as a complete item. Another, by the assistance of a second watch-glass, and two temporary brass hands, contrived to sell his watch twice, while keeping the most valuable parts of the works in his own possession.

The standard article of food used by the greater part of the population of India is rice, this grain being sometimes distilled into a liquor called arrack, sometimes ground fine and made into very white loaf bread, but mostly boiled and eaten whole. Sometimes fish and sometimes butcher's meat are eaten with it, and notwithstanding the heat of the climate, which one would think would induce the natives to eat nothing but the most cooling diet, they usually mix hot spices to such a degree as proves very disagreeable to the uninitiated palate.

The Chinese usually convey their food to their mouths with chopsticks, implements somewhat similar to ladies' curling irons. As these are not adapted to lifting much at once, they supply this defect by putting the dish close to their mouths and throwing in the supply with great rapidity, and do not set it down until their mouths are empty. Indians, however, merely use their thumb and first three fingers, with which they jerk their food into their mouths with exactness and dispatch.

In these warm climates, men have a much greater number of enemies to annoy them than in the more temperate regions. The first and minutest, though not the least troublesome, is the mosquito, something resembling a midge. On the wing it makes a noise similar to a bee, but considerably fainter and more shrill. As soon as the shades of night set in, they begin their depredations, and woe to every inch of human skin exposed to the attacks, especially that of newly-arrived Europeans, whose face, after sleeping ashore the first night, may be so disfigured as to be scarcely recognisable by his most intimate acquaintances. The next is the tarantula, an insect resembling a spider, but considerably larger and hairy like a mouse. Then the centipede, eight or ten inches long, scarcely as thick as the little finger, but with about twenty feet on each side. The scorpion is an unsightly reptile two or three inches long, with a tail nearly of the same length. Sometimes when it is touched on the back with a pointed piece of wood, the scorpion will turn its tail to sting what it feels touching it and will sting itself to death; there are also snakes brought aboard in hollow parts of fireworks, and these two are very dangerous. The cockroach, a large brown fly, is very troublesome by flying in the face and preventing or at least disturbing sleep; rats and bandicoots are animals nearly alike, who I have known leave the marks of their teeth in the thick skin of men's toes when asleep, and on one occasion to draw blood. In order to keep down the number of these vermin, it was the daily task of each boy on the ship to produce either a rat, a bandicoot, a scorpion, a tarantula, centipede, twenty cockroaches, or twenty eggs of this last named.

In these climates, bathing is very gratifying to Europeans but, from the dangers attending it, can seldom be enjoyed. If we go overboard from the ship we are exposed to the greedy jaws of the shark, and if we go in from the shore, to the alligator. Sometimes, however, a large sail is suspended by its four corners from the ship's yards, while the middle is allowed to sink a few feet below the surface of the water. This way risks are avoided and advantages enjoyed.

While refitting here, it was found necessary to quit work on deck at eleven in the morning when dinner was piped, and not to resume until two o'clock in the afternoon, the admiral thinking these three hours being too hot to work in the sun. Notwithstanding these, and many other precautions, the change of climate and a still more liberal use of arrack, toddy, and rich luscious fruits, to which the stomach was not seasoned, carried off a considerable number of our hands, many of whom were the stoutest men aboard. For myself, while in Pulopenang I had hurt one of my ankles. I did not first pay any attention to it, but what with climbing trees, running on sand, and bathing in salt water, it grew worse and worse, insomuch that on our arrival at Bombay, to which we sailed on 28 January 1805, it occasioned my being sent to hospital.

Bombay is one of the three principal settlements of the British in India. This town is considerable in size, regular and handsome, and is built on a small island of the same name, separated from the mainland by a narrow strait. There are two commodious docks on the island, and two or three more in preparation, the removal of the earth from these new docks being performed by women carrying it in small baskets on their heads. Shipbuilding here is performed in the docks and not on stocks as in England. When we arrived, a 74-gun ship was in considerable forwardness. The shipwrights here perform in a manner which in European estimation seems very awkward. A handsaw, an instrument thought absolutely indispensable by Europeans, is little known here. They use a small tool which serves as an axe, an adze, a hammer, and a mallet and more, and with this, and a chisel or two, perform the greater part of their work. All their boring is done with drilling instruments. The cutting across of a plank, which an Englishman would do with a saw in two minutes, takes one of them six or eight, besides losing three-quarters of an inch in length and leaving one end of the wood ragged and bevelled.

The harbour itself is large and tolerably commodious, with a great variety of vessels of every construction, from the English line-of-battle ship to the Chinese junk and the Malay prow. On board many of these small vessels from Persia and Arabia, the crews morning and evening pay their adorations to the rising and setting sun, and though we lament to see men worshipping any of the creatures instead of the great Creator himself, we would do well to imitate them in the regularity and fervency of their devotions

It was here I first saw public money changers. They sat side by side outside houses in the street with their tables covered with all the coins of the various settlements in India. A person leaving this port for any other could go to these changers and have their cash converted into the currency of the place to which he was bound.

Having been sent to hospital in Bombay, I stayed about a fortnight but reaped no benefit. I, and a few others who had been sent ashore with me, were taken back on board that we might attend the King's Hospital when we reached Madras, as the hospital in Bombay belonged to the East India Company.

In our passage to Madras, our admiral touched at nearly all the ports on the Coromandel coast by way of introducing himself, and seeing the situations of the different harbours. Everywhere we met with the most flattering receptions. The Portuguese settlement of Goa was more than ordinarily kind, and sent off, as a present to the ship's company, such a large supply of yams, mangoes, guavas, and other fruits, that our decks were fairly lumbered.

Goa is one of the finest and most delightful settlements in India: an excellent harbour, a soil teeming with fertility, an abundance of excellent water, and scenery to tempt a hermit from his cell, as well as genial a climate as can be found anywhere within sixteen degrees of the equator, though what signify these blessings if the machinations of man prevent our enjoyment of them. The Inquisition, worst of all evils, reared here its grisly head: that fiendish institution with its myrmidons of spies and informers, priests and familiars, and with all its train of racks, tortures and dungeons, with its secret, cruel, mysterious and vindictive doings that would blight the fairest prospect under heaven and convert a paradise to a pandemonium.

On these sea passages exposed to the salt air, my wound grew daily worse. So that one morning, when I went to have it dressed, Dr Fleming took me aside and said to me, 'I can do nothing more, and to prevent worse consequences, it will be necessary to take it off.' As I could not relish the idea of hopping home to Paisley on one leg, after some thought I concocted a brief pathetic address, which I knew would be nonetheless effectual in being delivered in a homely Scots accent. This, accompanied by a few tears, helped produce the desired effect. The doctor was moved to pity and promised he would have me sent ashore in Madras, which happened on arrival in May 1805.

At Madras, an entire new scene presented itself. There is no harbour at this place, and the ships lie in a very open and exposed road. For several miles to the north and south of Fort George, a low sandy beach presents itself, on which heavy surf continually breaks. Even on the calmest night, when there is not a breath of wind to agitate the waters, still the surf breaks onshore with considerable violence and produces a noise that may be heard a mile or two inland. Through this surf no English-built boat dare venture. The uniform practice is when an English boat approaches the shore with passengers, it anchors at a short distance from the surf until a native boat from shore comes out, these vessels being known as massulah boats. In these vessels there is not a single nail used, rather they are sewn together with small cords made from the bark of the coconut tree used in conjunction with wooden pins. They are not generally very tight or seaworthy, but as the passengers sit on an erection some distance from the bottom, they are not generally inconvenienced. These boats are about eighteen to twenty foot long, six to eight broad, and five or six deep. Their bottoms are flat so they remain upright when they ground on the beach.

As soon as the passengers are taken aboard, which, where ladies are concerned, proves pretty amusing to the tars, the boat proceeds cautiously towards the surf, the steersman, who, instead of a helm, uses a clumsy oar, singing a stanza or two of a native song. At every eight or ten words he makes a pause, and all the rest of the crew join in a short chorus generally sounding like 'ey-yaw'. The steersman stands on the highest part of the boat as it is of the utmost importance to enter the surf at the proper time, and when he wishes his crew to increase their exertions, he increases the velocity of his song, and the favourable moment being descried, the whole raise their voices in the most discordant notes, then, plunging their oars into the water with the utmost rapidity, raise themselves on their feet and then bend back their bodies with all their weight to give more force and efficiency to their strokes. A few moments of such violent exertions send them safely through the outer surf. The song then moderates until the boat draws near the inner surf, where the same process is repeated. The end of all this is a sudden, smart shock as the boat grounds. The crew leap out, which lightens the boat a little, and with the next surf the boatmen's shoulders bring her still further up shore. The passengers are then carried out in the arms of the boatmen and, before they can find them-selves recovered from the wonder of the scenes just witnessed, are safely on terra firma.

Sometimes, when people of distinction are in the boats, they are accompanied by one or two catamarans lest any accidents should occur. That is, if the massulah boats overset, the crews of the catamarans, who are expert swimmers, will rescue any passengers. Besides which, rewards are offered, and preferment promised, for the saving of the life of a European. When such claims happen, the catamaran man will seize the European before his clothes dry and recollection fades of his recent deliverance, and remind his saviour that he is a poor man who would be very glad to drink the massa's health. As the beach is generally lined with spectators, the slipping of the hand into the pocket, and the bestowing of its contents on one's rescuer is the only way to get honourably quit of such an affair.

I was no sooner set down on the beach myself, than

a handsome black boy accosted me saying, 'You want shampoo, massa?' I did not know what shampoo meant, but finding it would only cost me a single *fanam*, of which I had a few, I agreed. I thought it would be some article to eat or drink, or perhaps some natural or artificial curiosity. On signifying consent, he pulled out a little sharp instrument like a turner's narrow chisel, and set to work on the nails of my fingers and toes, pressing the skin back to elongate them as much as possible, and then reducing each to five, smooth, even flowing curves, that would have satisfied Chesterfield himself. He then took out another little instrument, like a surgeon's probe, on the end of which he dexterously fixed a little cotton, and began his boring operations on my ears, as if he were going to open out a direct communication between the two of them. But so lightly did he turn his muffled drill, that he touched the drum of the ear as softly as the distant purling of some mountain streamlet. He then pulled out a razor, but fifteen summers had not produced sufficient down on my chin to render him having to use it. Then something was wrong with the cut of my hair, and he took out his scissors and made everything right in that respect. Conceiving that all was over, I was about to pay his claim, when he seized my fingers, one after another, and jerked them until he extracted a crack from each. Then my ears received a few gentle pulls by way of securing better adjustment. Finally, he took my head between his knees and, fingering the veins of my neck a little, he gave such a twist as to make it ring. Now 'shampooed', I paid my single *fanam*, and received afterwards a European, a grandee, and a nabob salaam as change.

10. Madras naval hospital: May-November 1805

AS SOON AS THOSE of us who were destined for hospital landed, palanquins, a kind of carriage similar to a sedan chair but carried on men's shoulders by means of a long pole passing longitudinally through it near the top, were provided for us, and in these we were conveyed to the hospital. This lay a couple of miles inland and consisted of several rows of buildings called wards, one storey high, forming a large hollow square. These wards were about sixteen to eighteen feet wide, along each wall were placed couches for the sick, about eighteen inches apart, with the foot of each couch pointing to the middle of the ward, leaving a space of about six feet wide for a passage.

The square enclosed by the wards was laid out as a green plot ornamented with trees and shrubs. Parts of this enclosed garden were set aside as places where patients might walk. On one side of the space was a pond of rainwater which, although stagnant, was nowise noxious. In this pond those who were convalescent were permitted to bathe, and it is there, notwithstanding my wounded ankle, I learned the art of swimming. In one corner of the square was placed the general cooking house, and a neat bungalow in the English style for the resident surgeons.

Our diet here was tolerably good: bread and milk for breakfast, beef and mutton alternately for dinner, which dinner was accompanied by an English half pint of wine, or, in some cases, the same quantity of spirituous liquors. Supper was boiled rice, after the partaking of which a glass of peppermint water closed the day.

The head physician was Mr Underwood who visited the hospital daily, usually about nine in the morning. As soon as his carriage appeared, the cant words 'Ball up' were uttered and signalled that all stragglers should repair to their couches and compose their countenances previous to the doctor's visit. Some, indeed, who were scampering about the shrubbery a few minutes before, by the time the doctor reached them could not sit up to speak. But these shammers were pretty frequently found out, and sent back aboard their respective ships accompanied by a statement of their doings.

Mr Underwood was a man of mild aspect and great suavity of manners. He seemed to enter into the feelings and circumstances of each of the patients, and his goodness of heart did him much honour. He felt the pulses of the sick and examined the wounds of the lame, and prescribed to the two native assistants who accompanied him. Soon after his visit these assistants went round with medicines, plasters, powders, etc., but in the application of these, particularly remedies prescribed for the wounded, everyone might apply what seemed to him to agree best with his own wound, and many who were tired of the climate deliberately kept their wounds from being healed that they might be sent back to Europe. A sure means of achieving this was to bind a piece of copper on the wound, but this infamous practice was frequently detected, and, with great justice, severely punished.

On the couch next to mine was a Port Glasgow man called Bill Saunders. Bill was a capital scholar and a man of sound and enlarged reviews. Where Bill picked up all his learning I never learned, but a large stock he had, chiefly in the exact sciences. At this time algebra was his hobby horse, and wherever he went cantering I was at liberty to mount and follow behind. I went to work diligently, and in a few weeks the terms used in discussing involution or evolution, infinite series of surds, simple and quadratic equations, converging series, etc., became as familiar as household words. But it was too tiresome to everlastingly discuss the problems of x and y. Besides, although this might put something in our heads, it put nothing in our pockets. So we entered, like many another, a concern making straw hats. The method was this. After getting about a dozen or so ready, a native boy was dispatched on board some of the ships in the harbour to sell these hats. But often these boys would run off afterwards with the price, so we sustained more losses than gains.

These natives who were employed as servants in the hospital were considered by the rest of their countrymen as an inferior rank, and as belonging to the pariah caste. Notwithstanding, many were remarkably strict in their religious prejudices. I saw one of them, when a sailor by way of a frolic rubbed his mustachios with a piece of pork, plunge headlong into the pond and remain underwater as long as he could hold his breath and afterwards perform a variety of purifying operations. I have also known them to break the earthen cooking dishes (chattys) when they discovered that a European had used them. While on applying to one of them for water, I have frequently found it necessary to place my two hands sideways together, fingers pointing upwards forming a kind of funnel while they held their vessel a foot above my head and poured the water slowly into my hands.

These people, like the Egyptians, have a great variety of gods. Almost every animal that can be named is adored and worshipped and protected by some sect or other. One day I caught a beautiful lizard, and was amusing myself in examining its motions and colours when I was perceived by one of the natives. He approached me in great haste and perturbation, beseeching me to do it no harm as it was one of his gods, and if he were witness to it receiving some hurt without striving to prevent it, some great evil would befall him. This watchful care over their gods was sometimes converted by the seamen into a source of revenue. The members of the Brahman caste deify a species of bird something resembling our hawks, kites so voracious that they will sometimes swoop to snatch a piece of meat from a dish carried on a boy's head, even from his hand. One of these kites one day followed a cook boy into the very ward itself, where it was taken prisoner. The incident was reported to a Brahman who quickly repaired to the hospital and, after a little niggling about the prize, paid a rupee (about 2s 4d) and the kite was set at liberty. The usual method of catching these birds is as follows: a blanket with a stone appended to each corner is spread on the ground, in the middle of which blanket a piece of beef is secured. When the kite sees the beef he darts down, seizes it in his claws, and attempts to make off. Generally, however, he dips so deep into the blanket that his claws, being much hooked, get entangled, and he thus becomes an easy prey.

When any seamen died, a number of his shipmates were permitted to attend his body to the grave. This privilege was always eagerly embraced, as the cemetery lay about a mile off and the road to it passed several rackedowns (grog shops) at which it was a uniform practice to 'heave to'. An inside lining, as it was termed, was always the first concern and the second, if funds admitted to it, was a quart or two in bladders to smuggle back to friends in the hospital. For although no spirits were officially allowed into the hospital, a great deal of smuggling was carried on. This practice, coupled with that of buying one another's allowance of wine, enabled many to get intoxicated daily, and scenes of uproar and confusion, more fitting Bedlam than a hospital, frequently ensued. For those not particularly interested in these type of amusements some read, some wrote, and some indulged in the happiness of doing nothing but eat and sleep.

I remained in the hospital five months until 1 November, at which time I was sent back aboard. But the sea air disagreeing as ever with my ankle, it was soon infected again and, with the exception of a few short intervals, continued ill all the time I remained in India, and never became completely sound until I arrived back in Europe. The wounds of Europeans in warm climates being generally very difficult to heal, one cannot be too careful to avoid them or, if not, to treat them with immediate attention in the early stages.

11. HMS *Culloden* again – servant to Edward Hawke Locker: November 1805

ON MY ARRIVAL BACK on board, I found that Mr Dunsterville had obtained a situation onshore at one of the ports on the Malabar coast, and Mr Crease a lieutenancy in some other ship. To the first piece of intelligence I was indifferent, but the last was very acceptable as I cared not what promotion Mr Crease had, as long as he and I did not come into contact. I found, however, that previous to his departure he had taken care to prejudice all his brother officers against me. Even the petty officers seemed tinged with his prejudice, so that instead of one bitter enemy, I had a host of more moderate enemies. Their dislike of me was, to be sure, at second-hand, but the variety of its sources was fully equivalent to its decreased virulence. No duty could be too oppressive, no service too vile, no punishment too severe for me. I was compelled to wash swabs, sweep decks, turn spits, and every other duty requiring hard labour to which degradation was attached. My fortune, in short, was now at its lowest ebb. But while I was at the bottom of fortune's wheel, what is certain is that this wheel is ever in motion, and any change must be sure to lift me a little.

So it happened. At this time the admiral's secretary, Mr Locker, who had for sometime resided ashore, now came aboard and was allowed a boy to attend him. What induced him to choose me, black as my character was, I know not, but will merely state that his choice happily fell on me. This was announced to me while I was turning a spit on which was transfixed a young porker. The handle of this instrument was to leeward, and its fire, newly kindled, was rolling volumes of smoke into my eyes, while a boatswain's mate threatened me with a salute of scaldings should the rotary motion of the young grunter under my charge be not performed to perfection.

The person who informed me of my change of fortune was a Mr Young, master-at-arms, a cruel, piratical knave, and a base time-serving sycophant. Assuming an air of familiarity and kindness, he told me with a consequential look that he had been exerting himself in procuring a good situation for me and, what was better still, had succeeded in doing so. He expressed his sorrow at seeing me so oppressed at the spit, though he well knew that he himself was one of those who had put me there. Dissembling in my turn, I thanked him warmly for his exertions on my behalf, and told him I would continue to try to cultivate the good opinion he entertained of me. At this, he released me immediately from the spit, assisted me to wash, gave me his pocket handkerchief to dry my face and, in short, performed all those little services that one who was really my friend might have rendered.

As soon as I was cleaned and dressed in my best clothes, I waited on Mr Locker. Edward Hawke Locker would, at this time, have been about twenty-eight years old. In person, he was below the middle height and remarkably agile. His countenance was mild, affable and engaging. He possessed such presence of mind and coolness in the midst of action that under those various crosses, taxations, and disappointments which so readily take over other men, his features remained unchanged and serene. Though a certain suavity of air invited the approach of all, yet there appeared in his countenance a kind of dignity which repelled improper levity and all familiarity. His parts, naturally strong, were well cultivated by a liberal education richly improved by study, and highly polished by frequenting the best company. His taste in the fine arts was chaste and correct; he drew landscapes and views with great truth, and could make such an exact likeness of the human figure, even with his pencil, that anyone who knew the original would immediately recognise the subject. He was an admirer and good judge of poetry, and as plays were frequently acted on board, he once wrote a poetical prologue adapted to the occasion. He was also a sincere and pious Christian. The motto honouring his coat of arms was 'Fear God and fear naught', and under this motto his conduct was regulated. His dress was always in a plain manner, but with great neatness. In his capacity as admiral's secretary, the communications from all parts of India centred in his bureau. All naval correspondence with Europe passed through his hands, and as this was usually sent home in duplicate or triplicate, it will be seen he did not lead an idle life.

Even so, after the departure of Mr Dunsterville, he took it upon himself not only to read prayers, but also to deliver many valuable discourses and sermons. To introduce a high tone of morals among the crew, to eradicate ignorance, drunkenness, and swearing were objects with him, which he prosecuted with unwearied zeal and no small degree of success. So highly did the seamen respect him, that none would utter an oath within his hearing, or come across his hawse, as it were, while 'half slewed'. And while his station on board did not permit him to have much to do with the seamen in an official capacity, they were all closely united to him in terms of respect and esteem. Even I shared some of their goodwill, merely because I was his servant. Even his dog, Dasher, had many kind offices shown him, an instance of which I will now relate, although strictly this was far from being a kind office.

The seamen, being one morning ashore in Bombay, resolved on paying their accustomed visit to the local rackedown. Dasher, knowing them shipmates, joined the party, following behind on their expedition. Initially, he was shut out but they, hearing the scraping and whining noise at the door, opened it to find it was their shipmate. One of the seamen decided that the dog should not sit outside the door while he himself sat within, nor that Dasher should want a bite or sup while he himself had a shot in his locker. Dasher was accordingly placed at the head of the table, and compelled to take his glass in turn until the whole united stock of cash was expended. By this time Dasher was completely intoxicated and was compelled to be left under the table in the care of the landlord whose instructions were to give Dasher what he wanted when he awoke, being told 'Do not spare the expense, and we will square yards with you the next time we are in your creek.'

It was from my first meeting with Mr Locker that I date the commencement of what little mental improvements I have attained. Mr Locker had at sea with him a pretty extensive and well-chosen library to which I had free access. But as I was used to reading so hastily, without ruminating on what I read, I might be seen to reap from this a very slender advantage. However, reading the letters of learned and ingenious men gave me a relish for, if not knowledge of, good composition, and having some relish for poetry, I sometimes tried my skill in composing short pieces, in imitation of Mr Locker; would that I had been more solicitous to imitate him in more important matters. As he had done, I wrote a prologue to suit a play to be acted aboard. Then, I thought what I wrote good, but having looked it out again lately, now pronounce it as wretched a piece as ever issued in the name of prologue, lacking common sense, grammar, and over-loaded with expletives, feeble, confused and incorrect. However, never doubting its reception, I sent a copy to the manager, whose skill in poetry, I suspect, was of a piece with my own. He did not reject it on account of any of the above-mentioned faults, but returned it to me in a cover on which was written the following verse:

Would you be open to a friend's advice,
And sneering ridicule keep far away,
Note this, your orthography should be nice
Ere you can write fit prologue to a play.

Whoever heard such nonsense! For, if rightly spoken, how would the audience know whether or not it was rightly spelt? But the rebuff was not lost on me. After paying some attention to the spelling, I revised the piece and showed it to Mr Locker. The part I liked best (a compliment to Mr Locker himself) he gently drew his pen through.

Mr Locker knew that I loved to go ashore and was kind enough occasionally to procure for me this indulgence. On these occasions, I cannot say I had an inclination to drink spirits, but have mentioned before the incident of the seamen's making when Mr Locker's dog, Dasher, was intoxicated for the love they bore his master, and now found them disposed to treat his servant in a similar fashion. I was ashore, and fell in, by chance, with one of our boat's crews. Immediately they saw me, Jeff Peacock roared out, 'By all the powers, here is Locker's boy, Robert Hay; let us take him in tow, and if we do not bouse up his jib, he has never had it boused up in his life.'[38] They mounted me on their shoulders, as if chairing a newly-elected member, and off they went hurrahing to a rackedown. So closely did they ply me with fruit, sweetmeats, and arrack, that in a few minutes, I was not in one whit better condition than Dasher had been. I became insensible, and to this hour know not how I got back on board. I only know the next morning I found myself in my hammock with my face, shirt, blankets and pillow all smeared with blood, occasioned by the forefinger of my left hand having been split nearly in two from the middle joint to the point. I suppose it must have been placed on the boat's gunwale and jammed between the boat and quay, or the ship's side on coming aboard. Fortunately, some of the seamen kept me from the sight of the officers, a service which a fellow-feeling induces them in every possible case to perform for each other, and thereby I escaped the lash, which surely would otherwise have been inflicted.

My master, seeing my finger bound up, naturally enquired the cause. I felt I did not dare dissemble, and therefore made a candid confession. He seemed much surprised, as he had never observed in my conduct any symptoms of this vice. He represented to me the fatal effects produced by drink in its wretched devotees.

'It will assuredly, Robert', said he, 'dissipate the fortune, impair the health, injure the character, blast worldly prospects, and what is of infinitely greater moment, destroy the soul of all who addict themselves to it.' He concluded his remarks with the following story.

'A man was once offered by the great tempter all he wished, provided he would commit one of three sins. Namely, to murder his father, ravish his mother, or get drunk. He chose the latter, in which state committing the other two.' Since then, I have since erred regarding drink, but never without feeling subsequent regret and remorse. The young man, Jack Peacock, who had been the means of leading me into the scene of inebriety previously described, had no such mentor and no check on his conduct but fear of punishment, a feeble shield to ward off the darts of temptation, and being hurried along by his passions, a short time later fell a sacrifice to intemperance.

12. Mutiny at Vellore – capture of a French ship: July-September 1806

WE HAD GOT SOME intelligence of a French fleet expected in India and set about fitting out the ship for its reception, in the full hope of giving a good account of ourselves should fortune throw them our way. But while these operations were going on, we were, about 11 or 12 July 1806, greatly alarmed by a hasty message that came off from Fort George, ordering all our marines ashore with the utmost dispatch.

We found an insurrection had recently broken out among some natives of the interior, headed by some of the generals who had formerly served under Tippoo Saib, and who were now committing great depredations on European property. The report continued that the natives had already put an English garrison to the sword, and were putting all Europeans to death without distinction or mercy. This gave us much more concern than the report of the French fleet.

Once ashore, our marines instantly took over garrison duty, while the soldiers of the garrison were marched inland against the rebels – if rebels they could be called who were fighting to restore their ancient laws and institutions, and wresting the patrimony of their ancestors from the greedy hands of violent, haughty, and avaricious usurpers. We later learned that some instructions had been issued regarding the equipment of the native soldiers in the garrison of Vellore, which seemed to interfere with their caste system and then, being incited by the native captive princes being held at Vellore, on the morning of 10 July 1806 had risen to mutiny. After stabbing the sentinels, they had then levelled their pieces at the English soldiers as they lay asleep in the guardhouse, sending the greater part of them into a speedy eternity. Out of above two hundred men, not more than sixty were saved. These, in the general confusion, retired to the ramparts in a position over the gates of the city, and owed their safety to the earnestness with which the sepoys now began their work of pillage.

In the meantime, notice of these fatal events reached Arcot, about forty miles away, home of the nearest English garrison. The messenger had the good fortune to meet Colonel Gillespie, commander at Arcot, on his way to visit a brother officer at Vellore. The gallant colonel flew back, ordered the Arcot garrison under arms, and leaving orders for them to follow, set out in advance with a small squadron of cavalry. Little more than an hour after meeting the messenger, Colonel Gillespie was before the gates of Vellore. Initially, he found them impossible to force. Inside, the mutineers, satiated by this time with plunder, were now preparing to immolate the little party over the gate, who, having neither officer to command, nor a single round of ammunition, were beginning to flag, calling out piteously for that help which seemed impossible to afford. At this juncture a piece of rope was spied near the gate, the end thrown up to the party above, and by it Colonel Gillespie gained the ramparts. The scaling of a wall by a single rope should form part of a soldier's exercise. Now under an officer of determined bravery, the drooping spirits of the little party revived and they bravely defended themselves until a couple of gallopers arrived, forced the barriers, and gave entrance to the troops. A dreadful retribution now awaited the mutineers.

Shortly after this insurrection, we left the mouth of the Ganges, to return to Madras. We fell in with a French privateer, the *Emiline*, from Mauritius, which had been lurking about in the hope of picking up some of our Bengal ships. She had first taken us for a merchantman, and was preparing to throw herself alongside to carry us by boarding, but descrying her error before she came within range of our guns, she made off. We gave chase and soon gained on her, but she knew where her advantage lay, and kept edging inshore. About dusk, a shot from our bow chasers nearly reached her, but we had by this time shoaled water to five fathoms, and were constrained to abandon chase. The privateer herself grounded but, expecting a visit from our boats as soon as daylight should appear, she threw her guns overboard and by the use of her oars escaped. Next morning, we again got sight of her, hull down, and once more made sail. What scheming was employed that day to get more speed! All hands were first sent forward carrying a couple of double-headed shot, and then back aft. In both cases, the log was carefully hove, and as being down by the stern seemed to give a greater advantage, all guns and shot boxes were in a few minutes snugly stowed aft in the gun room. Now every inch of canvas was spread, and gangways knocked out to give the ship play, and every other scheme by which we might expect to get an additional fathom out of her. Before midnight the Frenchman was under our lee quarter, with his topsail to the mast, calling out in good English 'Don't fire, I strike! I strike!'

13. I join the carpenter's crew

AFTER WE HAD BEEN a year or two in India, our admiral identified a considerable want of shipwrights and caulkers. To remedy this he intended to appoint several boys to learn these branches, particularly the latter, for in England, contrary to Scottish practice, they are quite distinct. The carpenter of the ship, Mr Forbes, a countryman of my own, was the person under whose care the boys would be placed. This man frequently remonstrated to me the folly of a lad at my size remaining a 'shoe boy', a term of reproach for an officer's servant.

'How much better', said he, 'to leave Mr Locker and learn the shipwright's business. Then you would be rated one of the carpenter's crew on the ship's books, rather than a boy. A trade by land or sea, that would be of the utmost service in your life.' His reasoning seemed both plausible and solid and nothing but love for Mr Locker could prevent me from yielding to it. But at last the increasing importunities of the carpenter prevailed, and with downcast look, I requested my master's permission to leave his service. I did not tell Mr Locker I intended to learn the shipwright's business for Mr

Forbes had commanded me not to do so. I merely told Mr Locker that while I remained a servant I would be rated only as 'boy', and that I wished to do duty as a seaman. Mr Locker did not seem in the smallest degree offended, but acknowledged my reasons were sufficiently strong to induce me to make the request.

He was just then going to reside at Fort George, and after reiterating the advices he had formerly given me, he procured me liberty to go ashore, gave me permission to call on him, and furnished me liberally with pocket money. A few days later I availed myself of his kindness and called upon him at his office, where he charged me to let him know when he could render me any service. Emboldened by this, I solicited his good offices with the admiral to have me placed under the care of Mr Forbes to acquire some knowledge of carpentry. Mr Locker's promises were always more remarkable for their faithfulness than fervency, and this one was soon fulfilled. On my leaving him, he presented me with a pagoda (a gold coin of about 8s 6d value).

My attention now was given to acquiring the ready use of the axe, adze and caulking irons. In this, there was a good deal of opposition from the London caulkers. In London, the shipwright and caulking business are kept quite distinct, and it is nothing to find an excellent caulker from the Thames who can scarcely make a tool box himself or put a handle on his own mallet. In Scotland matters are managed differently, and the man who would pretend to be a tradesman because he could handle a mallet expertly, while he knew nothing of the use of the axe and adze, would be laughed at, as would a man who had set up as an author because he could make a pen or write in an ornamental hand. But Mr Forbes took care to have us boys initiated in both branches, and as naval discipline was too strict for the London men to make either opposition or remonstrance, they had to content themselves with styling us as 'double daubers'.

The greater number of repairs to warships in India were executed by carpenters and caulkers from the admiral's ship, who were sent on board other ships in small parties as need required. This subjected the carpenters to frequent changes of officers and situations, disliked by many, but to me, somewhat fond of change, quite agreeable. Furthermore, as a result of this we were in the way of witnessing and performing a great variety of operations, thereby improving our own knowledge apace.

Besides being sent to other vessels, we were sometime sent ashore to work, the making of masts and yards and the repairing of boats being our usual tasks. This everyone liked. In cases where we worked upon warships, the men had a rupee (about 2s 4d) per day. As learners, we boys had half this sum, besides our regular wages going on, and when we worked on merchant vessels, double this sum. Carpenters, therefore, were much better off than seamen, and though we had more expenses as regards clothing and tools, yet those who were anyway careful were seldom without money.

Ashore we had excellent shade to work in, and our hours were from six in the morning until six in the evening, with two hours for meals. After quitting work, we had two to four hours at our disposal, during which we might bathe in the surge, walk about town, or sit over a glass of arrack. It seemed to us the very essence of liberty, and we much regretted the summons to repair back on board.

In addition to all these enjoyments ashore, we had, at a moderate price, a plentiful supply of an excellent cooling beverage called toddy, procured from the coconut tree. This tree, off which there is a male and female variety, grows to a very considerable height and the stem is quite free from branches until a few feet from the top, where there are branches that are as soft as cabbage stems, and which spring out in a nearly horizontal direction. It is on this part of the stem, where the lower branches jut out, that the nuts grow. To procure toddy, an incision is made towards evening on the underside of the branch pretty near the stem of the tree. Beneath this incision is slung an earthen vessel called a chatty, which remains suspended till morning. The toddy exudes from the place where the branch is pierced, sometimes in such quantities that half a gallon is obtained from one in a single night.

The trees, having a long smooth stem, are difficult to climb, but the natives adopt the following plan. They take a piece of soft rope, between six and twelve feet of length, pass it round the tree and round their backs below the armpits. The two ends are then fastened together. Another piece of rope, but shorter, is passed round the tree and applied in a peculiar manner to the ankles. The operator, with his arms stretched out, lays hold of the rope with a hand on each side, pretty near the tree. Being in a posture ready to ascend, he slides the upper rope as high as he can up the tree, leans back his whole weight on it and draws his feet up the tree so that his knees are breast high. He then leans his whole weight on the foot rope, checks the other one up as before, and thus proceeds until he reaches the top. He carefully removes the chatty, slings it over his shoulders, and descends with equal expedition and safety.

A boat may be built of this tree, ropes and sails being made from some parts of the bark. The nut can provide food, and the milk drink. So a short coasting voyage might be made solely by the use of this tree and its produce.

14. In action against the French and Dutch: November 1806-February 1809

As the French possessed no other ports in the Indian Ocean than Mauritius, they could not uphold a large naval establishment, and but a few of their ships of war were placed on that station. A great many French privateers, however, were fitted out, which succeeded in making very numerous captures, privateers that were even known to attack the ships of the East India Company, although in these cases they were usually beaten off. We ourselves succeeded in taking two of these privateers and a great many more, together with a few regular warships, were taken by the different cruisers in our fleet. Although the French had such a slender footing in India, yet we had another enemy to content with, much more considerable. The Dutch, with whom we were then at war, possessed the whole of the fruitful island of Java, the ports of which served not only to fit out and protect Dutch warships and privateers but also offered invaluable protection to the French, allowing them to prepare their ships, and to recruit their stores.

It was against this island that the attacks of the

British in 1806, under Sir Edward Pellew, were directed. As the success of our expedition depended a great deal on secrecy, while we lay at Madras not the smallest information was given to us of our intended destination. We knew, indeed, from preparations that an attack was meditated somewhere, but this was all. A great number of fireballs were made, muskets, pistols, pipes, cutlasses and tomahawks were put in effective condition, and as soon as we got to sea we exercised daily at the great guns and with small arms. Soon after, enquiry was made whether any person on board had ever been in the harbour of Batavia, which we knew to be the object of our attack. Our fleet at that time was a powerful one. Eight line-of-battle ships, *Culloden* (74 guns), *Powerful* (74 guns), *Russell* (74 guns); three frigates, *Belliqueux* (64 guns), *Terpsichore*, and *Drake*, and a gun brig, *Seaflower*.

Approaching Batavia, we succeeded in capturing a Dutch merchant vessel, from whom we took a pilot well acquainted with the harbour. As he was an enemy we had reason to doubt his fidelity, but having no pilot of our own we were compelled to risk him. As an inducement to him a liberal reward was promised, to be paid as soon as all the ships of the fleet were safely anchored. On the other hand, on the binnacle was placed a pair of loaded pistols, the contents of which he was assured should pass through his brain should the ship go aground. Choosing between ample reward and instant death, he, on 27 November 1806, carried us safely into Batavia harbour.

In order to deceive the ships lying in harbour, we had approached under French colours, but they had either got intelligence of us, or strongly suspected us to be wolves in sheep's clothing, for, before we reached them, they either cut or slipped their cables and ran ashore. As soon as we came to anchor, boats from every ship were dispatched with a view of cutting out or setting fire to some of these enemy vessels, and in spite of some smart fire from the batteries ashore, we soon succeeded in boarding several.

The moment our sails were handed, a signal was made for all boats to repair alongside the *Terpsichore*, she and the *Drake* having anchored a couple of cable lengths inshore from us for the purpose of covering the attack. In a few minutes the boats were ranged into three divisions, the points of attack were assigned, and off they pushed in dashing style. Our first attempt was on a fine new frigate called the *Phoenix*. As the boat appointed to lead the attack, under Captain Pellew, drew near it, one of *Phoenix*'s great guns was observed pointed directly at it, a person standing at its breech with a lighted match ready to fire. In this critical juncture, one of our marines levelled his piece and shot him on the spot, otherwise our boat would undoubtedly have been sunk and probably the whole crew would have perished.

Nearly the whole of the *Phoenix*'s crew had previously gone ashore in their boats, and after this shooting the few individuals left jumped overboard, so by the time our men boarded there were none left to offer resistance. Our boarding party began by turning the *Phoenix*'s guns on some smaller vessels belonging to the enemy, and then we on the *Culloden* had the inexpressible pleasure of seeing a Union Jack at the mizzen peak of the *Phoenix*. For a considerable time we entertained hope that the *Phoenix* would be got off and watched narrowly to observe her changing position. But she had grounded too fast to be removed. At last, volumes of smoke curling up her masts announced her approaching fate. Flames succeeded smoke and in a few moments her whole masts and rigging were enveloped in a devouring blaze. Ship after ship followed in rapid succession and, ere night had fallen, the grand and sublime spectacle presented itself of seventeen or eighteen vessels being consumed by fire. Several of them were partly laden with spirits, which increased the brilliancy of the flames to such a degree that a small volume could be read on board the English ships three miles away. At intervals came the roar of the mortars as the enemy ashore attempted to throw shells aboard the English fleet, then the masts of the burning ships falling with a loud crash, and the still louder and more awful explosions heard and seen as the fire reached the powder magazine of the different ships – all heightening the grandeur and adding to the terror.

A day or so later a flag of truce passed between fleet and shore, though we private seamen knew nothing of the conferences. We did learn that the admiral had expected to find in Batavia a couple of line-of-battle ships, which he knew to be somewhere in the eastern seas, and was greatly disappointed to find they had left harbour some time before. While these two ships remained at large, our China ships were exposed to great hazard, and the admiral was determined if possible to find them and conduct them to a British harbour, or send them where he had sent scores of others, to Davy Jones' locker.

On 1 December 1806, leaving a couple of ships to intercept what enemy merchant vessels might appear, we set out on our return, passing through the straits of Banca, Singapore, and Malacca, at which last place we arrived on New Year's Day. In the whole of this expedition, only one man of the admiral's ship was killed, and three or four wounded.

The following year we again steered for Java, taking with us a transport or two and a small land force. We did not this time touch at Batavia, as we received intelligence of some Dutch vessels being at Cressy. On 20 November 1807 we sailed from Malacca, and wanting to pounce on them as speedily as possible we took the shortest passage, and narrowly escaped striking on some sunken rocks near Pedro Branco that were not laid down in our charts, still pushing our way through the straits of Banca as expeditiously as an intricate passage and baffling winds and currents would allow.

Cressy is a tolerable good harbour after it is gained, but the entrance, with numerous shoals, is somewhat difficult. On one of these shoals, below the bar, we had the misfortune to ground. This was a serious calamity as it prevented us from carrying on our operations with that degree of the celerity which in this, and many other cases, is conducive to success, and gave the enemy time to prepare.

Sir Edward sent his son, Mr Locker and Captain Burdett ashore with a flag of truce. These gentlemen stated to the Dutch commandant at Cressy, Mr Cowel, that we had come as natural friends of the Dutch, had no intention to destroy their settlement, and wished merely to clear the eastern seas of French warships. If such boats were in the harbour, if the Dutch would deliver them to us we would depart without offering any molestation, paying for our supplies in Spanish dollars. In return the Dutch commandant arrested our commissioners and sent them up the straits of Sourabaya and prepared to defend the town.

Sir Edward was not of a temper to brook this insult to his flag of truce, and therefore a concerted effort was put under way to refloat the *Culloden*. Boats were dispatched to take some of the coasting vessels sailing along shore. These were brought alongside and as many hands as could find room to work on board were immediately employed to cut out their decks and heave overboard their cargoes, preparatory to us stowing our guns and other heavy articles in these craft, that by this means we might be sufficiently lightened to float over the shallows.

The cargoes of these vessels consisted of an extensive quantity of goods for Europe from the Chinese markets: boxes of hardware, jewellery and porcelain, bales of silk, hogsheads of tobacco, indigo, gum, cochineal, packages of opium, sacks of yams, bales of cotton, bars of copper, steel, and iron, cases of ivories, elephants' teeth, cases and bales and casks the contents of which were unknown. All were thrown relentlessly overboard, and although strict watch was kept to prevent any articles from being brought aboard our ship, yet a considerable number of sailors made some valuable prizes, not least in their eyes being the extensive and variegated assortment of spirituous liquors they had on board, including a great number of cases containing one dozen square half-gallon bottles of rum, brandy, wine, gin, and arrack of excellent quality.

So great is the predilection of seamen to spirits that when it is assailed by temptation no consideration can induce them to practise abstinence. In the present case the certainty of speedy detection and punishment, the

consideration of being near an enemy's harbour, the
notice received that furnaces ashore were heating shot
for our reception, were to no avail. They knocked off
the necks of the bottles, and indulged, without
restraint, in copious draughts of the baneful and
insinuating potion. In a few hours there were some
hundreds of seamen intoxicated and unfit for duty.
Enraged, the admiral in the violence of his passion tied
up to the quarterdeck hammock netting on both sides
as many drunken sailors as could be ranged from the
break of the poop to the gangway, and the boatswain's
mates with their cat-o'-nine-tails were set to work on
them without mercy. But as this could neither whip the
gin out of them, nor render them fit for duty, so it was
of no service to proceed further with this measure, the
admiral swearing he would flog all hands as soon as
they got sober, and would never again hoist his flag in
a ship manned with such a set of drunken scoundrels,
and that every man of us would grow grey-headed and
rot in this country for not one of us should again see
Europe. He ordered his signal man to strike his flag and
with it immediately prepared to board the frigate
Caroline, telling us as he went down the gangway that
since no trust could be placed on us, he would share
the danger and honour of facing the enemies of his
country in the company of those on whom he might
place dependence.

This sentence stunned with remorse those of us who

were in a condition to listen to it, while our chagrin was even more augmented to see the *Powerful* (74 guns) passing at a short distance, her colours flying, her band playing 'Rule Britannia' and her gunners prepared to commence an attack on the enemy's battery.

Those of us who were sober, agitated by grief and shame, exerted ourselves to the very utmost to lighten the ship, and towards midnight we had the agreeable satisfaction of finding her afloat once more. The intoxicated, by this time having had a good sleep, were again at their duty. Being told what had taken place, they too were greatly dejected and from now on every exertion (and the exertions of seamen when judiciously stimulated are by no means small) was put forward to make a plea for their former folly. Small anchors were run out and by these the ship was hove expeditiously ahead. By unwearying perseverance we had the happiness of finding ourselves at sunrise in deep water. Notice of this was immediately sent to the admiral, and at daylight he placed himself on the quarterdeck of the *Caroline* with his spyglass in hand to watch our proceedings. He held his watch to observe what time we took to place the guns back aboard.

'Only a minute and a half to that one,' said he to himself with great complacency, but loud enough to be heard. 'I will again hoist my flag in her as soon as the guns are all aboard.' To the joy of all hands he returned about the hour of breakfast when we immediately weighed anchor and, preceded by a frigate to take soundings, started directly for the bay. The *Powerful*, who had passed us so proudly the day before, had now herself grounded, and had the mortification to see us on the attack, while being unable to share the danger and fame.

A small battery on the larboard shore on the island of Madura opened a smart fire on our frigate, but when we got abreast of it and began to play our lower deck guns on it, we soon put it to silence. Our admiral now seemed in his element. His eyes brightened, his countenance became more animated, his voice more cheerful, and step more firm. Though he would forget our faults, he never, even in the midst of the greatest possible dangers, allowed himself to forget our comforts. Finding as we drew within a few miles of the town that it was past noon, he gave orders to pipe to dinner.

'Let the lads get their dinner smartly', said he to the first lieutenant 'and their grog, for we will soon have other matters to mind.'

When within cannon shot of the town, a few shell were thrown as if trying our distance, but the firing was not kept up, so we naturally supposed the enemy was reserving fire until we came to close quarters. A good battery of cannon, with plenty of ammunition, are of the utmost service in defence, but of themselves insufficient. They are merely the body of defence, but the soul lies in valiant and patriotic hearts, few or none of which were to be found at Cressy. On reaching the harbour, we anchored at about half the gun length from the shore, directly abreast of the town and, by means of the spring previously placed on our cable, held to broadside. As we still expected an attack, our lower deck guns (long thirty-two pounders) were kept manned, while the hands belonging to the upper deck gun were employed in hoisting out the boats. These then shoved off, and all hands were sent to the great gun, ready to pour a broadside into the town should any opposition be made to the landing of our troops. None was offered, so the troops immediately took possession of the fort which had been recently abandoned. The governor, we afterwards learned, was taken to Batavia, tried for cowardice, and shot. The arsenal, the public store, and other places of note were taken possession of, but not the smallest instance of pillaging the inhabitants was either allowed, or seen.

We remained here some days, then, after getting a large supply of livestock and vegetables aboard, we sailed from Cressy with the satisfaction on our minds that there were not now in the eastern seas any ships capable of offering serious annoyance to our India or China trade, and during the year 1808 had merely a few straggling privateers from Mauritius to look after.

I still continued under the charge of Mr Forbes and, as he was assiduous in his instructions, I picked up such a knowledge of the carpenter business that in my subsequent wanderings proved highly advantageous.

In 1809, our appointed time in the east expired, and our thoughts and wishes all turned towards home. Early that year we put our ship in dock at Bombay, for such repairs as were deemed necessary to carry her to Europe. The successor to Sir Edward, Admiral Drury, had still not arrived, but after spending a few weeks preparing for our departure, we delivered up our authority. On 14 February 1809, accompanied by a pretty large fleet of Indiamen, and after dancing round the capstan to the tune of 'Off She Goes', we ran up our anchor smartly to the bows, and sailing from Point de Galle, on the island of Ceylon, shaped a course south-westward, uttering our last adieus to the spicy groves of India.

It will perhaps be thought that before leaving India I should give some account of the general features of the country, the manners, customs, religions and laws of the natives, the state of British power, the means by which so small a force keeps so large a territory in subjection, and many other topics upon which a man of observation would be able to descant. But it must be remembered that I was nearly the whole time on shipboard, and had no opportunity of enjoying either personal observation or judicious information on these topics, and that I was but a giddy, thoughtless boy, and had neither the wisdom, nor inclination to attend to them, and it is certainly better to be altogether silent on a subject, than to dwell on it in a manner that displays alike both ignorance and presumption.

15. The voyage home: 14 February-10 July 1809

DURING OUR PASSAGE TO the Cape of Good Hope, which took about six weeks, we encountered the severest gale of wind I ever experienced. Indeed, many of the older seamen aboard declared they were never exposed to such a storm. It commenced on 15 March, and raged all that day and the ensuing night. We continued to shorten sail, reef after reef, until on the 16th our topgallant yards and masts were with great difficulty brought down on deck. Additional lashings were put upon all, and our boats and great guns all double-breached and storm-cleated. Great care must be taken of the ship's guns in a storm for if one should break adrift, it is with very great difficulty and danger secured. The heavy rolling and pitching also had a powerful effect in straining the ship, so that towards evening she became so leaky she needed to be constantly pumped. During such weather, it was in vain to think of cooking, so we were therefore under the necessity of eating our provisions raw. As night closed in the scene became dismal in the extreme. Our quarter-boats were dashed to pieces, part of our quarter-galleries were knocked off, while the mizzen topmast with part of the mizzen masthead was now laying in confusion over our starboard quarter where it had been carried away.

And as if these real dangers and fears which beset us were not enough, some of our seamen gravely affirmed that shortly after the commencement of the gale they had seen the *Flying Dutchman* cross our bows under a very heavy press of sail.[39] This, joined to the circumstance of a large flock of mother Carey's chickens having been seen skimming along near the surface,[40] and to the knowledge that near this same spot *Ramillies* (74 guns) with a whole crew had shortly before perished, augured, as they mysteriously hinted, no good.

We were now under close-reefed main topsail, scudding at a rate of fourteen miles an hour. Eight men were placed at the helm on deck and eight more below on the tiller tackles; pumping was continuous. In this state night set in and Sir Edward, with his usual attention to our happiness, ordered the watch to be relieved so that those who chose to do so might repair to their hammocks. The greater number availed themselves of this opportunity, justly remarking that if the ship kept up they would, by being refreshed, be ready for further duty, and if she went down, death would show them as much quarter in their hammocks as he would do on deck. As I had the middle watch below, I turned in, as it is termed, and slept as soundly as I ever did ashore.

The gale continued with undiminished violence, and seemed towards daybreak to blow all with ever-increasing fury. At sunrise on the 17th every succeeding wave, as it approached us with its towering, curling summit whitened with foam, looked like a huge mountain with a top enveloped in snow, threatening to overwhelm us. What greatly added to our fears was that the sternpost was discovered to be loosening, while we could neither heave the ship to, to ease her straining, nor jettison the guns overboard while she laboured so heavily. It was suggested to the admiral that the ship would be aided materially if the deck guns were thrown overboard, and he replied, 'I do not think it necessary: she will do very well, and what would become of the convoy if we meet an enemy?'

By now many had bidden a last farewell to their friends and messmates. Even our admiral, who had weathered so many squalls, seemed agitated. Even so, wherever anything of importance was going on, there he was sure to be seen, showing he was commander by the intrepidity of his movements and his presence of mind. Dressed in a short jacket, a pair of trousers, a small hunting cap, and without shoes or stockings, he went about infusing courage and fortitude into all, but I verily believe that he himself, in his heart, thought all was over.

Our main topsail was still set, and as our admiral
had been heard to express a strong wish that it were
furled, a number of seamen volunteered their services.
He admired their bravery, but it was a considerable
time before he could be prevailed upon to allow them
to expose themselves to such danger, for we every
minute expected the mainmast to snap. At last,
however, he consented and a sufficient number of men
were permitted aloft. Every possible precaution to
secure the sail was taken, but without effect. No sooner
were the sheets started, than the canvas began to flap,
and in a minute the whole of it was seen fluttering like
so many pigeons high in the air. The admiral, rejoicing
that all the men had reached the deck safely, took no
more thought about the topsail.

Had the gale continued another night we assuredly
would have foundered. But shortly after noon on the
17th it began to abate, and before sunset we had the
pleasure of hearing pronounced those three words so
musical to the ears of the storm-beat mariner, 'The
pumps suck.' That is, the water has been discharged
overboard, and the pumps now draw only air.

The swell, as is always the case, continued for several
days after the wind abated, but although this again is
a very dangerous situation, we experienced no more
casualties. Shortly after the commencement of the
storm we lost sight of every ship in the fleet, but after
our arrival at the Cape of Good Hope the others of the

convoy joined us one by one, except four vessels which had not yet reached Table Bay by the time we sailed, and which, we learned later, had foundered as they were too deeply laden with saltpetre.

Cape Town, when viewed from shipboard, seems to lie at the base of Table Hill and to be in danger of being overwhelmed by the impending perpendicular rocks that overhang it. But when viewed from the town, Table Hill, the perpendicular part of it at least, appears a considerable way off, while the intermediate distances are occupied by tea and pleasure gardens which throw a healthy and cheerful appearance over the whole scene. Previous to a storm, the flat summit of Table Hill is frequently enveloped in a white fog. This appearance is called 'the spreading of the Devil's tablecloth' by seamen, and is the signal to make all snug before the approaching squall.

The climate at Cape Town seems to be quite healthy and the air salubrious. The fruits of both the torrid and the temperate zones come to perfection. The wine is of pretty good quality and moderate in price, and the waters of the coast abound with excellent fish. As this place is a constant rendezvous for British ships trading to India, the produce of both Europe and Asia are always to be found in its markets. On the whole, it seems a place where, in easy circumstances, a sufficiency of temporal happiness may be enjoyed.

From here we sailed to St Helena, where we arrived

on 8 May 1809 after a fortnight of more stormy weather. Our stay here was but short, and though our passage from India had been pretty quick, a ship came into harbour two days after us, bringing letters for our ship from Europe. These letters had arrived in India about the time we sailed from there, and had been dispatched after us by this ship that made a still quicker passage than we did. Amongst these letters was one for myself, acquainting me with the welfare of family and friends at home. As another ship was to sail to Europe two or three days before us, some of our men sent letters by her. I mention this that I might quote one written by an intimate acquaintance of mine, which for laconism could be hardly surpassed. After the date and the words 'Dear Brother', he simply added, 'St Helena, homeward bound, here I come. Thos. Moss'.

Shortly after St Helena we touched at the small barren island of Ascension where we got on board an abundant supply of turtle. The method of catching these is as follows: on the arrival of the boat ashore, the crew conceal themselves behind the rocks, as near the beach as possible, to watch for turtles coming ashore. As soon as one of these creatures is a little way from the water, one or two men rush from their hiding place, seize it by the side of its shell, and turn it on its back. They do not carry it to the boat, because they would be seen by other turtles, but just leave it in this position from which it cannot recover itself, and when they have as many turned as they want, they then carry them to the boat. In a few hours, our men took sixteen, the greater part of which weighed between two and four hundredweight. A few were kept in a couple of large tubs, purposely constructed, in salt water, which was renewed daily. The others lay on their backs at random about the decks, their eyes being washed every morning and a wet swab being kept under their heads, and in this state they lived until we made use of them, while some even survived until we arrived in England.

On one occasion, turtle soup, that distinguished dish of the voluptuary, was made for the whole ship's crew, but turned out a very sorry experiment, the seamen ridiculing it with a phrase in common use among them, that God sends the meat, but the Devil sends cooks. The officers, who had got ready the mess in kindness to the crew, and even sent some bottles of wine to mix with it, as is usually done, were somewhat nettled at the sarcastic remarks of the crew, and took care never again to repeat the treat.

The head of one of these creatures is remarkably disproportionate to the body, the head of a turtle which weighs in whole two or three hundredweight not exceeding an equal number of pounds. As for retentive-ness of life, I have seen a head that was separated from the body at six in the morning bite a piece of wood so closely as to be suspended by it twenty-four hours later.

They are amazingly productive. In some that were killed on the passage, we found upwards of one hundred eggs. These are not oval and brittle of shell like the eggs of fowls, but are circular, of an orange colour, and coated with a tough skin, a wise provision of nature to prevent them from receiving injury when deposited for hatching in the sand.

Our passage from this island was pretty favourable, and early in July 1809 we took soundings in the British Channel. It would be difficult to describe the sensations which pervaded our minds. The recollections of wives, children, parents, brothers, sisters and friends rushed with intense pleasure over the mind. Even those who had no relatives to excite such pleasure cast their thoughts back to the days of youth and the endearing scenes of their nativity.

The lead used for trying the depth of water is hollowed out at its base, and this hollow filled with grease in order that some part of the seabed may adhere to it, thereby showing the nature of the sea bottom. At our first cast, a few particles of coarse sand came up. These were carefully picked off by one of the officers, and put into a glass of wine, with which, after giving it a violent shake or two as if to imbue it with the soil of England, he drank 'happiness and prosperity to our native land.' All our favourite national songs were chanted that day with great good humour. One, 'Then Sling the Flowing Bowl', in which occur the lines 'Bear a hand, be steady boys soon we'll see/ Old England once again' was chorused and encored till the decks were made to ring.

16. Arrival in England and shore leave: 10 July-6 December 1809

IT WAS ON 10 July 1804, at six in the morning, when we sailed from Spithead for India, and on 10 July 1809, about the same hour, we cast anchor in Cawsand Bay, Plymouth. The practice of giving seamen, on their return from a specified number of years of foreign service, one third of their wages, and a fortnight's liberty to visit their friends, had lately come into use, and all of us entitled to this gracious treat obtained leave from 1 to 15 August.

My friend Robert Wright and I, intending to visit Scotland, remained in Plymouth only one night, proceeding next morning by stagecoach to Tavistock. Our purpose was to proceed northwards to the Bristol Channel, in some port of which we expected to get on board a vessel bound to Scotland or, if not, we still expected to get a passage across to south Wales where we could proceed to Scotland by land. On passing Knackers Hole, a tollgate three miles out of Plymouth, where soldiers are stationed to intercept deserters, we were very strictly examined, but Wright and I having our passports, were permitted to pass. Another shipmate, William Arrol, who was bound to Barnstaple, having had the misfortune to lose his passport was stopped. The united testimonies of Robert Wright and myself proving ineffectual, our poor companion was dragged back as a deserter to Plymouth.

We dined that day, 2 August, at Tavistock, and afterwards set out on foot for the village of Sourton, which we reached a little before dusk. Having had for many years little practice in walking ashore, we found ourselves greatly fatigued and after washing down a comfortable supper with a glass of first-rate cider, we strolled out for an hour to examine the village. An antique church and burying ground adjoined the village, and we repaired thither to see what mottos could be found, and to indulge in the perusal of other memento mori. The first that met our eyes was one that is found in almost every country churchyard in England: 'Afflictions sore, long time I bore / Physicians tried in vain, / Till God it pleased that death me seized / To terminate my pain.'

Shortly after midnight, a rap was heard at the door of the house in which we slept, and an enquiry made whether or not two seamen had taken lodging there overnight. Before giving an answer, our landlady with great prudence came to our bedside and acquainted us with the circumstance, adding, 'Should it be anyone you wish not to see, you can easily effect your escape by a back passage.'

As we could not guess at the reason for such an ill-timed intrusion, we desired our hostess to admit the visitor, but we were somewhat agitated. We had just time to arise and clothe ourselves when the stranger came bouncing to our bedroom door, and who should present himself but our shipmate Arrol, who on his return to Plymouth had called at the house at which he had first slept and there found his passport wrapped up in a pound note. The soldiers had immediately granted him his liberty and he had set out after us. He was half seas over,[41] as the phrase goes, and was, at his best, not noted for his veracity, so we could not believe one of his many contradictory statements. We were glad, however, of his company, for he was a very humorous fellow, knew the country well, and promised to introduce us to good lodgings at Barnstaple where he had served his apprenticeship as a ropemaker.

The distance from Sourton to Barnstaple is upwards of forty miles, which to any of the sons of Neptune is a Herculean task and although we took the road early in the morning, being so little accustomed to travelling our feet soon became blistered. We stripped off our shoes, placed one in each stocking, the mouths of which we tied together and threw them across our shoulders and carried them. About twilight we reached Barnstaple. Our first care was to inquire whether there was any vessel in the harbour bound for Scotland, and found to our great mortification that a vessel loaded with fruit had sailed for Greenock the preceding day, but no other was due to sail for Scotland for several weeks. Surely, we thought, man is born to disappointment as well as trouble. Since we could not reach Scotland, our next wisest step was to make ourselves as comfortable as possible in England. With this view we repaired to an inn, kept by a Mrs Davols, the former mistress of our travelling companion. Here, over a good warm supper, a few glasses of excellent toddy, and a dish of chit-chat with the two bewitching daughters of our hostess, we half forgot our disappointment and chagrin.

Next morning we set out for Ilfracombe, a small village skirting the Bristol Channel, in the hope of getting across to Wales, but again were disappointed. No decked vessel would sail for the sake of two passengers and, as it blew pretty fresh, neither would any of the open boats venture out. In pensive mood, and with reluctant steps, we retraced our way to Barnstaple. The following day, preferring motion to rest, we commenced a journey to Exeter, at which place we took a coach to London.

In this great national emporium we spent three days, our bed and board for which time was 10s 6d each. The architectural appearance of this great city fell far short of the ideas I had formed. But this was more than compensated by the opulent magnificence that everywhere met the eye. The wet docks were full of shipping, while the bosom of the river was so studded with vessels that one would have thought it impossible that the watermen's boats, gliding along everywhere, should be able to procure a passage across the river. The streets in the vicinity of the docks were so crowded with porters and carmen that it was with great difficulty we could stir afoot. What a busy anthill this would seem to one removed from it by a perpendicular mile or two. How many thousands of millions of its tiny inhabitants had been consigned to its sepulchres since this huge city first reared its infant head as a Roman colony? And in how few years must every individual who is now stirring about with such bustling activity be consigned to a dreary tomb.

But I am wandering from my subject. The rapidity with which our funds were ebbing compelled us to confine ourselves to exterior curiosities, but we did not see one-twentieth that were worth our observation. I did, however, seek one object which, to me at least, possessed greater attractions than all the curiosities of London, and this was the face of my old and valued master, Mr Locker. Wright and I called on him at his house in Berkeley Square, and were received as old shipmates with all the kindness and affability for which this man was so distinguished. He gave me permission to write frequently, and when we took our leave, presented me with an elegant copy of Watt's *Improvement of the Mind*, and some volumes of Pope's works. The first mentioned book (notwithstanding a shipwreck and many other disasters) I still have, a book I value very highly on account of its own intrinsic merits and, of course, still more highly from the esteem and affection I bear towards the giver.

When our time was nearly expired we again mounted the coach box and, without being beholden to wind or tide, anchored in Plymouth on the night of 14 August 1809. When I had quitted the ship I had received £14, and although I considered I had been pretty economical, at the end of the fourteenth day I was reduced to my last shilling. Few of my shipmates, however, could boast of such economy, many of them having gone through double the sum in half the time. Liberty being so precious, we determined not to give up a single hour of ours, and slept that night ashore. Next day, 15 August 1809, we repaired, as ordered by our passports, on board the receiving ship *Prince Frederick*. From that ship I was in a few days turned over to the *Salvador* on board which I had so often been, and for which I entertained such an inveterate dislike. I continued on board of her, with the exception of a few intervals in which I was sent with others to assist in fitting out different ships, until 7 December when I was sent to join the *Amethyst*, frigate.

17. HMS *Amethyst* – we are wrecked and I run away: 7 December 1809-16 February 1811

THE STATION OF THE *Amethyst* was the coasts of France, Spain, and Portugal, where we were employed to reconnoitre in the enemy's harbours, cutting out vessels, and in destroying, for we rarely succeeded in capturing, the chausemarees, or luggers, they employed in the coasting trade.

On one of these occasions we chased a small vessel until we were in range of the guns from the shore batteries of France, which took care to attempt to make us feel the weight of their metal. But though the fire was pretty brisk, only one shot fell aboard. Passing over the heads of a numerous group of men standing on the quarterdeck, it went through the two upper decks before dashing William Martin, a young Irishman and messmate of my own, into a dozen pieces. His flesh, as I collected the scattered fragments, creeped to my hand as if unwilling to part.

I have heard it frequently asserted that cannon shot could not be seen while flying in the air, but on this occasion I saw several, not only those we fired but also those returned by the batteries. We did succeed in catching one vessel and found her loaded with salt. We sent one officer and a few men aboard to take her to England, but she grounded on a small island off the coast of France and was lost, although the crew were saved.

The pleasantest time I enjoyed while I belonged to this ship was spent on the small island of Howat, off the south coast of Brittany, where I was sent with a few others to break up a small French coaster, the *Bertha Catharina*, for firewood, which we slept aboard as it was lying on the beach. We had firearms with us and plenty of ammunition, so that we had the pleasure for an hour each morning and evening of roaming about the island shooting rabbits.

A few French families reside there, cultivating parts of the island, and these we easily kept on good enough terms. The men of these families seemed to live a very indolent life. They lay about the doors, while the women were busily employed at various departments of the agricultural business. I had an opportunity here of seeing the operation of thrashing in a way quite new to my eye, but which led back to thoughts of antiquity. Sheaves were laid on the ground in a circle of about thirty feet in diameter, the top of the sheaves pointing to the centre. Around this circle, not an ox, but a nimble pony trotted, briskly 'treading out the corn', while a little French maiden stood in the centre holding the reins and cheering its labours with a rural song.

I did not intend to make myself known by my trade when I joined the ship, but the carpenter was a Mr Snell, a sometime shipmate with me in the East Indies, who now applied to the captain to get me into his crew. I was rather surprised at this as we had never agreed when equals in rank, and now agreed still worse in relation of master and servant, so that my whole time on board was spent rather uncomfortably.

Towards the evening of 15 March, Captain Walton came on board and we immediately expected to weigh anchor. He, however, had instructions to carry some live cattle for the fleet in the Channel, and as night drew on without any appearance of the lighter with the cattle coming off, it was necessary to remain until the following morning. In expectation of putting to sea, we had, during the afternoon, unmoored ship, and were now lying at a single anchor. As our stay in Plymouth Sound was to be only one night, it was not thought necessary to again secure the ship. We simply gave her sixteen or twenty fathoms more cable and, as it was blowing now rather fresh, the topgallant yards and masts were struck. In this state, all being snug, a quarter watch was set and the rest of the crew retired to their hammocks.

During the first watch a gale blew up, and at midnight the wind came from the south-southwest with great violence. The night was also excessively dark, in which circumstance the drifting of the ship was not perceived. At midnight, when the watch was called, the opinion seemed that the ship had drifted considerably. High land under our stern seemed indistinctly to appear, to which was added the sound of breakers, more appalling to the ears of British seamen than the sound of an enemy's cannon. The alarm was given and all hands called. The first consideration was to let go a second anchor, but by now it was too late, for the white foam from the surge was seen at intervals twinkling through the gloom, and nothing could be done but to hope the gale would abate, and we could ride it out till morning. Such hopes, however, were of short continuance, for about a quarter past midnight a violent shock announced to us our speedily approaching fate. The second shock unshipped the rudder, when she almost immediately veered broadside on and heeled over nearly on her beam ends.

One part of a carpenter's duty is to try how much water is in the ship, and impart this information to the officer of the watch, that the pumps may be set going when need requires. I accordingly sounded a few minutes after she struck, and found three feet of water in the hold. I reported this to the captain and the pumps started, but by the time she got broadside the water had increased to five feet, and at that it was considered in vain to labour any longer and the pumps were abandoned.

Fortunately, the women had all been sent ashore the preceding day, so we had not their screams to add to the general confusion. With much difficulty the boats were hoisted out, and were immediately filled with part of the crew eager to gain safety. One of the boats, two or three minutes after she left the ship, was tossed aloft by a towering wave and precipitated with irresistible fury on the breakers. She was dashed to pieces and several men aboard sank to rise no more. In order to lighten the ship, orders were given to cut away the masts. This was promptly done, a few feet above the board, where they all fell with a tremendous crash. A number of seamen scrambled out onto the masts, to get as near the shore as possible and so have a shorter distance to swim, but several were washed off and swept away. The cries of those perishing were truly heartrending. We heard occasionally their feeble voices, supplicating that help which, alas, we were unable to afford. As well, darkness excluded the helpless sufferers from our view and we neither knew how, nor where, to exert our aid.

The fury of the storm increased: minute guns were fired, blue lights were burned, sky rockets were let off and signals of distress continued to be made. This drew several boats around us but to grant assistance was out of their power, as to have come alongside would have been destruction to them. One captain of a merchant vessel, whose bravery and humanity overcame his prudence, perished in the attempt and thus, endeavouring to save the life of others, unfortunately lost his own.

All hands were now struck with consternation and dismay and everyone felt uncertainty and gloom. The officers, hoarse by so much exertion of voice, now issued their orders hesitatingly. Subordination, the first but most important branch of naval discipline, seemed suspended and every man now did that which was right in his own eyes. In vain did the captain call on all hands to remain on board till daybreak. The cries of the seamen, the howling of the tempest, the murky darkness of the night, the signals of distress, the roaring of the surge, and the screams of the dying, all added to the horror of the scene, making the whole both alarming and terrific.

Between three and four in the morning I went below, put on my best clothing, and took a few small articles which I most esteemed. Mr Locker's Watt's *Improvement of the Mind* was not forgotten. These I tied up in my greatcoat, and thus equipped went on deck resolved to make a try for the shore. By this time, one end of a hawser had been floated, and was fast to the rocks ashore, while the other end passed through a block attached to the bowsprit. On this hawser was placed a thimble from which a hatch was suspended, so as to traverse freely from ship to land. This hatch swung about so much as to intimidate the first person who made trial. He jumped off, and swore he would stop aboard the last minute, rather than trust himself on such a crazy machine.

I did not think much of it either, but saw no other way of gaining the shore, and therefore placed myself on the hatch, tying my bundle to it by means of a small line, so that if it were washed off I still might recover it. All being ready, I gave the word 'Ease away,' and so I did, flying between wind and water. I moved with considerable velocity until more than halfway ashore, where the bight of the hawser hung slack in the water. Now every succeeding wave went over me, and so twisted my bundle and the line as to prevent the hatch moving a single inch. I could not move nearer the shore, nor could those aboard pull me back. How long I remained in this perilous predicament I know not, hearing the voices from the ship crying on me to clear away the hatch, while those ashore were shouting, 'Keep up your heart, my dear fellow, and hold fast!' Had it been daylight, I am sure several people would have eventually ventured out to help me, but darkness magnified the danger to such a degree that no one would stir. At length, one of the seamen who had been impatient to get ashore came down the hawser, and when he reached the hatch, he cut the line with which I was so entangled and assisted me to disengage myself. We then plunged together into the surge, and in a few minutes reached terra firma and safety. Here we found a considerable number of people from the town. After receiving their hearty congratulations, we crossed the neck of land that separates the Sound from the harbour, loosed a boat we found, and crossed over to Plymouth. Here my companion left me, and I proceeded alone to the dock, where I arrived as the day began to dawn.

18. In Plymouth – I join the *Edward*: February-April 1811

GOING DIRECTLY TO THE house of a person who used to make all my purchases ashore, I found the husband had just gone to work while his wife was still in bed. But as soon as I told her my story, she sprang out and I jumped in, where, enveloped in good warm blankets, I soon buried all remembrance of the events of the previous night in sound repose. When I woke about noon, instead of finding myself in a ship of war, aroused by the morning gun, or the shrill sound of the boatswain's pipe, I found myself in a snug little parlour with no other sound in my ear than the soft, soothing murmurs of the teakettle, supported by the more substantial concomitants of ham, eggs and butter.

As the person with whom I lodged was connected with the dockyard, I had the opportunity of hearing the fate of the *Amethyst* and its crew. The former soon went to pieces, the latter were sent on board the guard ship. I never heard accurately how many perished, but believe the number was about thirty, one of whom was William Arrol, my former travelling companion.

Unfortunately, I could not be accommodated with a

regular bed at this house and therefore was necessi-
tated to take a bedroom across the street. This meant
slipping backwards and forwards between my
bedroom and my lodgings, a very dangerous practice
as press gangs were always on watch, for the house
was situated at North Corner and was not a hundred
yards from the beach. From the windows, which faced
the harbour, hundreds of vessels could be seen riding
at anchor in Hamoaze while great numbers floated
past with the tide. Watermen's skiffs, merchantmen's
yawls, warships, launches, pinnaces, cutters, gigs, etc.,
were every moment landing. Porters trudged along
under ponderous burdens, women of pleasure flitted
about in all directions watching for prey, Jews stalked
about with hypocritical gravity hunting the dupes, and
lastly, the jolly tar himself was seen with his white
dimity trousers fringed at the bottom, his fine scarlet
waistcoat bound with black ribbon, his dark blue
broadcloth jacket studded with pale buttons, his black
silk neckcloth thrown carelessly about his sunburnt
neck. An elegant hat of straw, indicative of his recent
return from a foreign station, cocked on one side; a
head of hair reaching to his waistband; a smart switch
made from the backbone of a shark under one arm;
his doxy under the other, a huge chew of tobacco in
his cheek, and a good throat season of double stingo
recently deposited within his belt by way of fending
off care: thus fitted-out, in 'good sailing trim', as he

himself styles it, he strides along with all the importance of an Indian nabob.

Had this sketch finished the picture, it would be agreeable enough, but the darkening shade of the press gang was always there, which damps all the enjoyment which sailors experience ashore. Merchant seamen, in particular, durst scarcely show their faces on the street. After the shades of night had fallen, and after taking courage with a glass or two of good Jamaica, they would sometimes sally out to take a ramble. But generally, as their spirits and courage rose, their prudence and watchfulness forsook them and many, very many, instead of finding themselves in the morning in the arms of Polly, would find themselves in the press room of a guard ship in the more unceremonious hands of a corporal of marines.

Added to this terror of deprivation of liberty, and a dread of being informed against for the sake of gain, was the further apprehension that I might be seen by one of the *Amethyst*'s officers. While in this unpleasant situation, I was one morning accidentally observed by an old East India messmate who, after exchanging a few hurried words, went to make my case known to Robert Wright. We had been separated shortly after our return to the *Prince Frederick*, he having been put aboard the *Valiant* (74 guns), shortly before I joined the *Amethyst*. The *Valiant*, having been fortunate enough to capture a French ship of great value, my friend's share of the prize money was sufficient to purchase his liberation from the Navy. He had obtained his discharge about the time I was shipwrecked, and when my case was made known to him was just on the eve of setting out for Scotland.

He flew to me on the wings of friendship, soothed my cares, quieted my apprehensions, animated my hopes, invigorated my resolutions and, what was no less necessary, replenished my empty purse. The crew of the ship which had lately returned from a foreign station had recently obtained a fortnight's liberty. As many would probably remain in Plymouth, and would not use their passports, my friend would strive to procure one that would suit my appearance but, unfortunately, this he could not manage.

He then offered to purchase me women's clothes, and take me with him as a wife, or to buy gentlemen's clothes for me and take me as his master, or to travel with me by night, concealing ourselves by day. Anxious as I was to return to Scotland, I thought it too dangerous to adopt any of these schemes as I knew, from my previous experience, the stiffness of the watch that was kept on all roads from Plymouth. Nor did I doubt that, subsequent to the shipwreck, still greater vigilance on the part of these 'man traps', as they were aptly called, would be displayed.

Robert also tried to procure me a berth in some merchant ship but here also his exertions were fruitless.

I could not allow myself to detain him long, he was losing precious time, and spending money that he wanted to carry him to Scotland. I therefore accepted from him £3 for which I gave an order to my friends in Paisley, although he had no expectation of receiving such an order when he gave me the money. I took this opportunity of sending a trifling present to my mother and sister. After many expressions of deepest regret in parting, and offering up our earnest wishes for each other's safety and prosperity, we tore ourselves asunder, each uttering as he threw a parting look over his shoulder a dejected and disconsolate farewell.

After about three or four weeks a waterman, whom I had employed to look out a berth for me in some ship, succeeded in finding one. I, too, dressed myself in a waterman's outfit and without delay went on board. I found the captain was ashore but the mate informed me they wanted hands, and that the captain would be aboard the following morning, when he had no doubt I would be engaged. I accordingly went back aboard next day, and after having answered a few questions touching my skills, was signed on for the voyage for £4 10s per month. The ship's name was the *Edward*, a new vessel of between four and five hundred tons built at Sunderland, but Bristol-owned, ballasted with coals, and bound for Jamaica where she was to take in a cargo of sugar, rum and coffee.

Her master, Captain Germain, was part-owner and

a hardy, active, and experienced seaman. He was hasty in speech, hasty in temper, and equally hasty in getting work done. He was seldom satisfied, even with the conduct of those who tried to please him, so that when he fell in with seamen of stubborn disposition there was a continual state of warfare. The provisions on board were of the cheapest, and not a drop of spirits allowed. Those of the seamen on board who were better acquainted than I with the general usage of merchant vessels were very indifferent to their provisions and treatment. For me, all was much better than I had been accustomed to in the King's service, but when the rest used to complain so would I, in order that I might hide my ignorance of merchant service usages.

The *Edward* remained in harbour about a week after I joined, during which time my mind was in a state of utmost anxiety. Our berth in Plymouth harbour was within a very short distance of the wreck of the *Amethyst*, so every small boat that passed made me tremble, as my fears placed one of the *Amethyst's* offices on board of her, and every moment I expected to be discovered and sent on board the guard ship as a renegade and deserter.

19. The *Edward* sails to the West Indies: April 1811

AT LENGTH THE LONG wished for, and at the same time much dreaded, morning arrived, and we weighed anchor about sunrise. It was April, the weather was exceedingly fine and the resplendent orb of day had just arisen on the horizon. On a mind not agitated with fear and apprehension, the scene was calculated to inspire joy. But what signifies all exterior happiness to a mind agitated with dread and terror? For it is the practice in British ports for the men-of-war to take a daily turn in rotation to send a boat aboard of all vessels which have just arrived or are preparing to sail, to inquire whence come, whither bound, and so forth, and to press any superfluous hands found aboard.

I thought it pretty certain that one of the *Amethyst's* officers would attend in this boat, and as all knew me well how could I escape? With what fearful emotions did I cast a sidelong glance beneath the foot of our foresail at the broken hulk of the *Amethyst* as we slowly passed her. I could not avoid contrasting the pleasures of this joyful morning with the horrors of that disastrous night in which I made my escape. To my surprise, no boat came alongside, the breeze freshened as we receded from the land, and in a short time we doubled the point which forms the south-west boundary of Plymouth harbour.

As a bird long confined in the cage feels on recovering its liberty, so felt I when I found myself in the open sea. One other ship (the *Medea*) left Plymouth at the same time and, being bound to South America, we kept company for a few weeks. When about to part, we closed to get an account of each other's reckoning, a practice quite common and very serviceable as regards navigation. We agreed on our latitude, which indeed was no wonder, as we had been but seldom deprived of our observations at noon, but in our longitude we differed widely, as she put herself eighty miles further to the west, and must have been that much wrong, for a few days after we made the east end of the island of Antigua, at precisely the time expected.

During our passage, our boats needed some repair. Our carpenter who had never before been at sea, and whose knowledge was confined to heavy ship work, knew but little about small boats. As I had been frequently employed on repairing such in the East Indies, I was (as the captain was pleased to allow) of considerable service.

As we approached Jamaica we made two very good stow holes for hiding those members of the crew who carried no exemption warrants from the press. What

with carpenter's warrants, apprentice's indentures, and
so on, all on board were protected but four of us. We
drew lots who should occupy the stow holes and I was
one of two left to stand on deck. My partner dressed
himself in greasy clothes, and blackened his face with
grease and soot, with the intention of passing as ship's
cook. I, with the assistance of some landsman's clothes,
dressed like a footman, and adopted an air of flippancy,
intending to pass as steward. As the cook is usually the
most useless man on board, and the steward generally
no seaman, by assuming these characters we hoped the
press would not think us worth removal. Fortunately,
we were not put to the test, for we passed Port Royal,
that hotbed of the press, about midnight, and the next
morning arrived at Old Harbour, where men-of-war,
or their boats, seldom visit. About this time, I cut my
foot so ill with an adze that I was unable to walk, which
later cost me a great deal.

On the outward passage, the seamen had been very
discontented. The ship was leaky, the hands few, and
the duty pretty severe. The ship, they naturally
assumed, would become still more leaky when loaded,
while the provisions, already bad, would grow still
worse. They had hitherto greatly irritated the captain
by their turbulence, and they doubted not that, on their
arrival back in Bristol, Captain Germain would not
only not endeavour to screen them from the press, but
on the contrary might, by way of revenge, betray them

to it. In addition, the seamen knew that wages of £9 a month for the run home could easily be obtained. So, although if they deserted they would forfeit the immediate wages due to them, they would not eventually be great losers.

When a West Indiaman first begins to take aboard her cargo, in this case sugar, it is the custom, though a very injudicious one, to hoist the first hogshead as high as the tackles will admit, and to leave it suspended until the crew take in a good stiff bowl of rum to drink success to trade. When our first hogshead was hoisted up, the men pawled the capstan, and requested that this custom be complied with. As it was pretty near dark, Mr Payton, the mate, begged them to at least get the boat clear, when they should immediately get this allowance. This request was perfectly reasonable, but as the crew would not yield, so the boat had to be cleared by a few Negroes. This quarrel widened the breach and, one after another as they got the oppor-tunity, the crew quit the ship. The last five, determined not to wait behind, one day forcibly seized the small boat, handed in their clothes, and forced two of the boys to go on board to row them ashore and bring the boat back. The cries of the boys alarmed the captain, who sprang into the boat himself, resolving by force to compel them to desist. But they had gone too far to retract, and when it came to physical force, what could two boys do against five stout and determined fellows!

After a short struggle, the captain was compelled to sit quietly and see himself rowed ashore against his will, in his own boat, by his own boys, under the insulting command of his own seditious, deserting crew. It is probable I would have joined them, for I had several reasons to be dissatisfied with this captain, and was moreover anxious to seek a ship (of which there were many in several ports of the island) bound for Greenock, but my foot not having yet healed from the adze cut, from necessity I had to remain on board.

Shortly after, our carpenter quitted the ship and, as a substitute in could not be easily procured, the captain proposed I should go home in that position at £7 a month. I was rather hesitant as I knew I was far from being fully qualified, and mentioned this as a cause of my scruples. He silenced me by saying he had seen on the outward passage what I could do, and if I were willing to try my best, he was willing to accept my services on the above terms. Therefore I agreed, and immediately began to perform the duties of my new station. We had no cooper on board, so this work naturally devolved to me, and what with repairing sugar hogsheads, superintending two Negro caulkers, plus many other items of duty, I was kept abundantly busy. I assisted occasionally in stowing the hold, and did not fail to leave a snug stow hole for myself as a retreat from the press gang.

Our seamen having left the ship, all our harbour

work was now performed by Negroes. These men will work the whole day at the capstan under a scorching sun with almost no intermission, beguiling the time by singing one line of an English song, or a prose sentence, at the end of which all the rest join in a short chorus. The sentences which prevailed with the gang we had aboard were:

> Two sisters courted one man,
> *Chorus*: Oh huro my boys,
> And they live in the mountains.
> *Chorus*: Oh huro boys, O.

and the second:

> Grog time of day, boys, grog time of day.
> *Chorus*: Huro my jolly boys, grog time of day.

Our captain, able now to get forward with harbour work, never looked for seamen until a cargo was nearly all aboard. As soon as new seamen joined, he took care to haul the ship a mile or so from shore to prevent their escape once they sampled the provisions and duty. The second mate and I were to keep watch all night to prevent this. The ship being so leaky, several hands believed she would never reach Bristol; a circumstance occurred which set them in some measure easy on this point, and which will also serve as a specimen of the superstitious beliefs held by the sons of Neptune. On my way to Chapeltown village to get some ironwork done, I found a horseshoe which I carried aboard and nailed to the foremast. One of the seamen, seeing me, came and shook me heartily by the hand and swore he would not now be afraid to sail in her, even if she were bound for Canton! But still so unhappy were some of our new crew, that two hailed a passing man-of-war boat one day, and voluntarily went on board! Our captain was greatly irritated and spoke to the coxswain of this boat very sharply for removing his men.

'You may save your cheek music, my brave fellow,' said the coxswain, 'If your whole crew had a mind to step into this boat of mine, I would take every man and mother's son of them, with never once a by your leave.' As it was, our second mate was pressed while ashore filling water casks, the captain requesting I should go ashore to fill the rest of the casks. This I did not wish to undertake, for although carpenter, I had no exemption warrant to show, and would be liable to be taken as well. Knowing, however, that he had no other hand he could trust for fear of running away, I complied and had the good fortune to return safely.

I would strongly recommend to every young man whose duty leads him to serve others, not to be too strict in having the precise limits of this duty defined, and abiding within these limits. In all my engagements, I have tried to render myself as generally useful as possible, and whenever requested to perform any service, have never stopped to inquire whether it fell within the lines of my engagement, but rather considered how I could perform it in a way best suited to promote the interest and satisfaction of my employers. This has often been the means of securing me the goodwill and confidence of my employers, thus smoothing down some of the asperities we are all more or less doomed to meet in life. It has more than once been the cause of my promotion, while at the same time it never subjected me to any heavier work. Those who show great anxiety lest they should go beyond their duty are generally called to do everything that can be placed within the line of duty, and are gainers of nothing but their employers' ill will.

20. The *Edward* sails back to England: July 1811

AFTER A FEW DAYS, our convoy being collected, we sailed for England under the care of two brigs of war. In sailing from Jamaica we do not, as many would suppose, steer a direct course. We first sail in a westerly direction towards Florida, then up the coast of America to the banks of Newfoundland, and from thence chart a course, with almost always a fair wind, easterly for the south end of Ireland, which we round to gain England.

Our homeward passage, if anything, was more disagreeable than the outward one. The convoy consisted of between seventy and eighty sail, of which we were by far the slowest, continually lagging astern. We were therefore forced, at all times, to carry all the sail we could possibly set. This not only subjected us to additional risk in shortening for a squall, but had a powerful effect on straining the ship, and thereby keeping us constantly at the pumps. Often, as night closed we would see the other ships in the fleet nearly hull down ahead, taking in their small sails, and preparing to run for the night under just three topsails and foresail, while we were still forced to crowd on every inch of canvas the ship could carry, lest the rest of the fleet be out of sight in the morning.

One day, about a fortnight out from Jamaica, we were greatly astern of the fleet, when one of the war brigs dropped back to hail us. Their captain told us that as we could not keep up, he found himself under the necessity of leaving us to make the best of our own way, as it would be an injustice to detain the whole fleet for one dull sailer. Germain was highly incensed at this. He told the warship captain that he would protest against such conduct the moment he arrived in a British port. He could not help the sailing of his ship, while it must be evident that he was carrying more sail than was consistent with safety. He added that our ship was very leaky and the number of crew small, and by leaving us to ourselves, the warship captain was exposing ship, cargo, and lives to imminent peril. And that if any misfortune befell us, he, the war-brig captain, would be made responsible. This remonstrance, which was made in a very spirited manner, proved effectual, the brig heaving the end of a hawser on board, and dragging us up to the fleet. After this, when we dropped astern, one of the best sailers was ordered by signal to take us in tow. On one of these occasions, when it blew very fresh, the ship that had us in tow was apprehensive of dragging us down and thought it prudent as she changed watches to let us go.

We, equally afraid, of being dragged under, let go at the same time. Of course, away went the tow rope. A few days later, when we got within hail of the same ship and requested her to drop the end of our hawser aboard, we finally got knowledge of the above events.

The crew on the *Edward* continued to get more and more dissatisfied with the amount of work, insisting on being put on the war brig. Our captain was (and with good reason) highly exasperated. At this time it was dead calm, but as soon as a breeze sprang up he urged his course towards the brig to oblige them. On this occasion, the boatswain and I interposed. We told how fatigued we were with incessant labour at the pumps, and if we lost three more hands it would be impossible for the rest of us to work the ship. Also, that if he acquired a reputation of putting his crew aboard men-of-war, it might prove highly disadvantageous to him when he came to recruiting a new crew. Finally, that in a few weeks we would arrive at Bristol, where he would no longer be troubled with the men in question. He admitted the truth of this and as we had previously prevailed upon the three refractory hands to show submission, matters were made up and work went on as before.

On the banks of Newfoundland a dense fog generally prevails, and when many ships are in company, it is necessary to ring bells, blow horns, fire guns and so forth to prevent them from running foul of each other. While there, we saw one very large whale within pistol shot, and an extensive shoal of porpoises but, having no fishing tackle, took no cod. We left Newfoundland with a good wind, and the night after we made Cape Clear on the south-east Irish coast every ship was left to make the best of her own way; we, of course, were left alone. We had, however, an excellent breeze and as our captain was by no means backward in displaying his canvas, we soon reached the entrance of the Bristol Channel, where we got a pilot aboard. Now the crew began to put on their airs of humility, while the captain, in his turn, assumed an air of determined arrogance. He would not listen to the proposal of putting any of them ashore down channel to escape the press boats, but determined that everyone should stand his chance.

As we proceeded, we passed within a short distance of Ilfracombe. At the sight of this village the recollections of past scenes crowded of my mind. 'Two years ago', said I in mute soliloquy, 'was I at that village eagerly seeking a vessel to cross the Bristol Channel on my way to Scotland. And now after all the dangers, fears and disappointments, I am still but little more than half a gunshot nearer the object of my fondest wishes.'

Having in our favour a smart breeze, and a strong tide, we soon lost sight of the village. Bearing in mind that part of the sailors' creed which forbids them to look further back than the end of the spanker boom, I soon forgot Ilfracombe, and as thoughts of the future were sufficient enough to occupy my whole attention, I was glad to let thought of the past slip away.

Unless the press is very hot, a carpenter's warrant is generally considered sufficient protection. But the captain not wishing to be at the expense of having one drawn up in Jamaica, I had none to show, there being only a verbal contract between us. Our pilot informed us that a previous ship had had the carpenter taken off. He had gone aboard one of the fleet to repair some damage and after finishing the job had begun to hand back his tools. At this, the press officer told him he need not mind.

'You are a handy fellow', said he 'and just such a man as we want. I will lend you a boat to fetch your clothes when more at leisure.' Although I might not merit the compliment paid to this carpenter I knew I might meet the same fate, and was prudently resolved to put more faith in my stow hole than either my verbal warrant or the press gang's mercy. We reached King-road, at the mouth of the River Avon, shortly after dusk, and were in hopes that we would remain un-observed till morning, by which time we might get ashore. After coming to anchor, seamen were sent aloft to furl sails. I was a few steps up the rigging to loan a hand, when I heard an Irish whisper from above, 'Carpenter! Down! Down! The gang are alongside!' A moment found me on deck hurrying to the aft hatchway. Before I could reach it, I found myself seized by the arm. I trembled.

'You are running right upon them,' whispered the boy who had called to me from the rigging, 'They are on the quarterdeck. Down the forepeak or you are gone!' I darted down like lightning into my stow hole, and in a twinkling found myself beneath two tiers of sugar hogsheads, and trembling like an aspen leaf. A moment or two later down came several of the gang.

'I see you, my old genius,' said one.

'And I see you, too, my young fellow,' said another.

'You might as well come quietly', said a third, 'for out you shall come!'

'Out here at once!' vociferated a rough, appalling, voice, 'Or the cutlass will taste your beef in a jiffy!' And on this they all began thrusting their cutlasses down to the hilt amongst the interstices of the hogsheads. Happily, I was more than a cutlass-length down, and besides, took care to let them have all the talk, and to breathe softly. After about half an hour, I heard the voice of the boy calling out the gang were gone.

I went up onto the deck to find that two men had been pressed. My great anxiety now was to get ashore, but the captain had gone to Bristol in the small boat, and would not be back before morning. We saw several other boats passing, but durst not hail them lest they proved to be the press. As it grew dark, two or three came near enough to be spoken with, but although the second mate, boatswain and myself offered half a guinea apiece, none could be prevailed to take us. They knew there was a guard boat prowling about, and if they were caught screening seamen, they themselves would become victims. At length, however, about midnight a boat passed close under our stern, and with her crew the three half-guineas overcame the fear of danger, and they consented to take us aboard. Now another obstacle occurred. The mate decided he would not allow me to quit the ship. 'You know', said he, 'her leaky condition, and that there are almost no crew aboard. Therefore, if any damage happens to the cargo, it will be at your risk.'

I told him the pumps were in excellent condition, and the ship would not make so much water as she did when labouring under oppressive sail, so that the boys could easily keep her dry until she hauled up the river. At this, a violent altercation took place. He and I had had several petty quarrels on the homeward passage and now he seemed to rejoice in this opportunity of thwarting my purposes. But no arguments would have been powerful enough to have dissuaded me from my point except force, and this he did not possess as the boatswain, second mate, and one or two others favoured me, so that we were more than a match for the mate and the boys. So taking our small stock of movables and, on my part, a small cask of sugar I had brought home as a venture, we jumped into the boat and pulled towards the harbour.

Just before we reached the harbour entrance, we were alarmed by the sound of oars. Our boatmen declared it to have come from the guard boat, and therefore changed our course and grounded us at the nearest point of land. Supposing it sand, we sprang overboard to find ourselves above the knees in mud. Fear lending us assistance, we soon succeeded in extracting ourselves from our woeful plight, but I dropped my cask of sugar, never to be seen again. Whether it sank in the mud, or was found by the guard boat crew who thought it a better prize than its owner, I never knew.

After jumping over, and scrambling through, many fields, dykes and hedges, we succeeded in reaching the village of Pill at daybreak. Here, at the principal inn, over some pork chops, new potatoes, and a bottle of good Jamaica, we soon forgot the disasters of the busy night. Here the second mate (Mr Lindsay) and myself met a family consisting of a husband, wife, and two very agreeable daughters. With one of these damsels Mr Lindsay fell deeply in love and I, in order to keep them company, paid some attention to the other. But several reasons combined to prevent us receiving much pleasure in this situation. The voyage had not been of long duration and although the wages were good, the sum due to us was not very extensive. My wages, in particular, were reduced by one month's advance received in Plymouth for £4 10s. But of this I got no good. I had had no time to get the order cashed before I left, and had given it to my landlady that she might have it in readiness for me when I should write for it on returning to Bristol. She, however, had received my instruction in a different light, and when I sent for the money and my books to be forwarded, informed me she was under the impression that the month's advance had been given her as a present, and she had used it accordingly, but that my books should be sent on. My books never reached me, so I lost both.

As to our ship wages, the captain alleged some rum had been pilfered on the homeward passage, the cost of which was to be made up in equal proportion from the wages of each of the crew members once the quantity had been ascertained. But as we were paying a guinea a week for our board and lodging, and to this adding our washing, drink, and other pocket money, our stock was diminishing with vexing rapidity. To add to this, we could see from my window the boats passing on the Avon, and my fears converted each one into a press boat. However, the house in which we lodged possessed one particular convenience. A little way up the vent was a concealed hole in the wall which enabled a person to hide himself above the ceiling of the room. This was originally used for smuggling spirits. Shortly before we were there, a seaman in a similar predicament had occasion to use this hole. At that time, a few kegs of gin were already stowed there. Betwixt a sailor and his drink there is at all times the attractive power of a needle and a magnet. This man contrived to start a bung, and had taken nearly a quarter of good Hollands beneath his belt, which soon laid him on his beam ends, when the press officer entered the apartment below. The seaman was by now snoring like a grampus, which greatly alarmed the inmates of the house, less the discovery of the gin (rather than the seaman) should take place. They, however, contrived a good deal of walking, calling after the servants, laughing, cracking jokes, etc., to drown the sound before it reached the press officer's ears.

There was an Irish girl in these lodgings, waiting with her parents for a fair wind to Cork. I am perhaps too grave now to expatiate largely on the exterior charms of the fair sex. Suffice to say she completely came up to, or far surpassed, any idea I had ever at that time formed of a beautiful and fascinating woman. I was something of a rhymester, and as love and beauty are standard themes to this tribe, I strung together some verses in praise of this enchanting Hibernian paragon. Then I thought them pretty good, but now, when distance of time has obliterated the subject of them in a great measure from my remembrance, I must confess my opinion to be much changed. I will not occupy room in transcribing the whole of my parting address to her, simply inserting the last verse as a specimen: 'From Britain's isle, I'd freely part, / In any clime to lodge, / Could I possess the tender heart / Of the adored Miss Dodge.'

After a few weeks we received our pay, but what with stoppages for the alleged pilfered rum, board wages, and commission to our hosts for acting as agent (for we did not dare venture into Bristol), great inroads were made into our funds. I immediately disposed of, to great disadvantage, my seaman's clothes, and purchasing a long coat, breeches, and other corresponding vestments, and assuming as much as possible the looks and gait of a landsman, I set out on foot for Bath, thence to take a coach for London.

21. By coach to London – the press gang – HMS *Enterprise* and HMS *Ceres*: September-October 1811

I SLEPT ONE NIGHT on the way, reaching Bath the next day at noon. As the London coach did not leave till two o'clock, I spent a couple of hours sauntering through the streets of that fine city. Many of the buildings and shops far exceeded in grandeur and elegance anything I had seen, but my mind was too intent on what was before me to give that much attention to these matters.

The outside passage money on the coach to London was £1, but this sum was considerably increased by the equally unjust, and importunate, claims of drivers and guards for refreshments. This practice is a great imposition to travellers, and connived at by coach proprietors and drivers who take good care not to let such a profitable business fall into disuse. My financial stock, therefore, on reaching London was sadly impaired. We reached the metropolis next morning at eight o'clock, my feelings being considerably different from what they were when entered by the same way (Hyde Park Corner) twenty-five months before, when I was still in naval bondage. Now my thoughts were raised by the idea of freedom, and my hopes excited at the prospect of embracing in a week or two those from whom I had long been separated. But if my hopes were high, so were my fears. One of my fellow passengers, hearing I was a stranger to London and intending to visit Scotland, offered to conduct me to the wharves where Scotch vessels lay. But I did not like his looks and, as civilly as I could, declined his offer.

Without stopping to breakfast, or to examine a single curiosity, I pressed forward in as straight a line as possible for the river. I had gained sight of the vessels' masts, and in imagination had procured a passage when, crossing Tower Hill, I was accosted by a person in seaman's dress who tapped me on the shoulder, enquiring in a familiar and technical strain, 'What ship?'

I assumed an air of gravity, and surprise, and told him I was not connected with shipping. At this he gave a whistle, and in a moment I was in the hands of six or eight ruffians whom I soon found to be a press gang. They dragged me hurriedly through several streets, amid bitter execrations bestowed on them from passers-by and expressions of sympathy directed towards me, until they landed me in one of the houses of rendezvous. Here I was carried into the presence of a lieutenant who questioned me as to my profession, and whether I had ever been to sea, and what business had taken me to Tower Hill. I made some evasive answers, but on my hands being examined, and found hard with work, and discoloured with tar, I was remanded for further examination.

Some of the gang then offered me spirits, while the scoundrel who had first laid hold of me put on a sympathising look, and observed what a pity it was to be pressed when almost within sight of the Scottish smacks. Such sympathy was well calculated to exasperate my feelings, but to think of revenge was folly. I was more concerned they would examine my small bundle, for in it there were a pair of numbered naval stockings, purser's issue, which would not only have made them suppose I had been at sea, but that I had been in a warship. I contrived to hide these, unobserved, behind one of the benches.

In a short time I was re-conducted for further examination before the lieutenant, who told me I might as well make a frank confession of my circumstances as it would save time and ensure me better treatment. What could I do? I might indeed have continued solid and silent, but whether or not such a procedure might have procured me worse treatment, the one thing it would not do was restore me to liberty. I therefore acknowledged I had made a voyage to the West Indies as carpenter. His eyes brightened at this.

'I am glad of that, my lad,' said he, 'We are very much in need of carpenters. Step along with these men and they will give you a passage on board.'

I was then led back the way I came by the fellow who first seized me, put aboard a pinnace at Tower wharf, and by midday was lodged securely on board the *Enterprise*, where I was immediately sent down into the great cabin. Here there were tables covered in green cloth, loaded with papers, and surrounded by well-dressed and powdered men. Such silence prevailed, and such solemn gravity was displayed, I was struck with awe and dread. No sooner did I enter the door than every eye started on me, and as there might be some there who knew me, I scarcely dared raise my eyes. A short sketch of what had passed between the press officer and myself had been communicated to the examining officer who thus addressed me.

'Well, young man, I understand you are a carpenter by trade?'

'Yes, sir.'

'And you have been at sea?'

'One voyage, sir.'

'Are you willing to join the King's service?'

'No, sir.'

'Why?'

'Because I get much better wages in the merchant service and, should I be unable to agree with the captain, I am at liberty to leave at the end of the voyage.'

'As to wages', said he, 'the chance of prize money is quite an equivalent, and if you are obedient and respect your officers, that is all that is necessary to ensure you good treatment. Besides', continued he, 'you may in time be promoted carpenter of a line-of-battle ship, when your wages will be higher than in the merchant service, and should any accident happened to you, you will be provided for.' I argued, but under great disadvantage. My interrogator was like a judge on the bench; I like a criminal at the bar.

'Take my advice, my lad,' continued he, 'Enter the service cheerfully, then you will have a bounty, and be in a fair way to promotion. If you continue to refuse, remember you are aboard, and you will be kept as a pressed man and treated accordingly.' I falteringly replied I could not think of engaging in any service voluntarily when I knew of a better situation elsewhere. He said no more, but making a motion with this hand, I was seized by two marines with these words ringing in my ears, 'A pressed man to go below!'

My doom now being fixed, I was thrust down among five or six score miserable beings who like myself had been kidnapped and immured in the unwholesome dungeon of the press room. Such is the blindness of human nature! We are so often on the very brink of a precipice, when we think ourselves in the utmost safety, and dream not of impending danger.

By some mismanagement on the part of the purser's steward, I was left all day without food and water and would have been the second day also, but that two or three of the most humane of the seamen took me into their mess and applied for my allowance of provisions. With the exception of these few, I was generally treated with ridicule and contempt. Seamen who have been pressed together into one ship usually have a great affection for one another. Their trade, their habits, and their misfortune are all the same and they become endeared by similarity of suffering. But my landward appearance placed me in some measure beyond the pale of sympathy. I was styled by way of distinction 'the gentleman', and considered a butt for their shafts of nautical wit and banter. This did not affect me greatly as I knew I myself had often joined in the same strain of irony against those being brought on board the *Salvador del Mundo* in landsmen's clothes. I was now merely being paid in my own coin.

Once or twice a day, a limited number of us were permitted on deck to breathe fresh air, but from the surly manner in which we were treated, it was easy to observe that this was not for our pleasure, but to preserve our health, which would have soon been greatly endangered with the pestiferous breaths and pestilential vapours of the press room. I remained in the ship something more than a week, when she became so crowded as to render the removal of a considerable number of us a measure of necessity. I, among others, was put aboard a cutter, closely confined, never seeing anything in our passage down river but the sky divided into minute squares by the gratings which covered our dungeon.

We arrived at the Nore shortly after dusk and were immediately put on board the *Ceres*, guard ship. I rejoiced at its being dark, because I thereby escaped the prying gaze of four or five hundred pairs of eyes, among whom some might have known me. The following day I blended in properly with this motley crowd, thinking it folly to dress any longer in landsman's clothing. I therefore purchased a second-hand jacket, trousers, and check shirt, and packed up my long coat, breeches, vest, white neck cloth, etc., lest I should need them on some future occasion.

Next morning, my acquaintances were greatly surprised to see how completely I had been meta-morphosed, not only in my external appearance, but even more so in my manners. Hitherto I had preserved the greatest taciturnity. I knew that had I talked too much, sea phrases would have slipped out. Hence credit was given me for far more wisdom, learning and politeness than I possessed. How easy is it to be thought wise? It is merely to preserve silence and though we may not thereby give an opportunity of displaying our wisdom and wit, we can, with greater ease, conceal our ignorance and folly. Now, being seen to be able to string together the technical terms of seamanship, I was on a footing with the rest. None of my shipmates knew my name except one, pressed shortly after myself, and who called to me as soon as he came aboard. This was one of the sailors in the *Edward*, one of those who had seized the boat in the West Indies and pulled ashore in spite of the captain's threats. Bill, Tom, Dick, Bob, Jack came all alike familiar to me, and when I knew I was spoken to I answered to all of them promiscuously.

In the ship we had liberty to go on deck at all hours, and were thus much more comfortable than on the *Enterprise*. Our distance from shore being only about six or eight miles, the land was seen very clearly, and many an anxious, earnest look did I take of it, forming in my imagination schemes how to gain it. The distance from the shore itself was no small barrier, but what made the attempt truly hazardous was that there was only one point where there was any probability at all of making a landing: the Isle of Grain. But how was this to be gained in the dark? And even suppose it gained, how could I escape observation in wet seaman's clothes? How could I travel anywhere without being intercepted? But even if these obstacles were surmountable – how was it possible to escape from a ship guarded by midshipmen, quartermasters, ships' corporals and marines? Even though any attempt to escape seemed impractical, I was constantly meditating upon the subject.

22. Escape: October 1811

AMONG THOSE PRESSED ABOUT the same time as myself was a man a few years older than I, a native of Hartley, by the name of John Patterson. I often observed him casting many a wishful look to the shore, uttering a half suppressed sigh as he turned his eyes from it. He, too, had doubtless observed my conduct, for he frequently looked earnestly at me. We soon came to be on speaking terms, though still abstaining from introducing the subject evidently close to both our hearts. Eventually, after many conversations, we opened our minds to each other and finding our sentiments in unison, we became inseparable. From this time, almost the whole subject of our thoughts and conversation was escape. But whatever view we took of the matter, the obstacles seemed insurmountable, and had the prize been anything less than freedom, we would have despaired of success.

'He', says the proverb, 'who thinks an object unattainable makes it so.' Our first consideration was how were we to get clear of the ship and reach the shore? We considered using inflatable bladders, and prevailed with one of the men belonging to the ship's boats to purchase them for us. We then tore up some old shirts and made them into long narrow bags, large enough to hold up the bladders when full-blown, and of sufficient length to go round the body below the armpits. Straps were attached to pass over each shoulder, and one to pass between the legs in order to keep all in proper position. We had seven bladders in whole, of which Patterson had three large and I four small, whereby our quantity of wind would be about the same.

At this time there were so many people on board that there was not room for all to sleep below. A considerable number, therefore, slept in the waist hammock nettings. A place on the upper deck projecting a little beyond the ship's side was where the greater number of beds and hammocks were stowed during the day. As both the sides and top of this place were covered with tarpaulins, Patterson and I slept there comfortably enough, and each night watched for a favourable opportunity of escape. Our destination would be Maldon in Essex where Patterson had been, and knew several of the captains of colliers belonging to the north of England. We expected that if we could reach Maldon safely it would not be difficult to procure a passage towards home.

Many nights passed after our resolution was taken, but before we were able to make the attempt. Some nights the tide did not suit, some nights it was too light, and on some a very strict sentinel was on duty. About

10 or 12 October 1811, I do not remember the precise date, conditions seemed to bid fair. The weather was dark and lowering, the wind blew pretty fresh, and all appearances promised a wet night. What was still of great consequence, the tide exactly suited us. Before dusk, we purchased and drank two or three glasses of rum each, that we might better stand the cold, bade adieu to a couple of our bosom confidants, then repaired to our station in the hammock nettings.

When the evening drum beat a little before eight o'clock, the drum and the storm made enough noise to prevent our movements being heard, while the sentinel who paced the gangway was fully muffled up close in his greatcoat. At this point, Patterson felt strongly inclined to draw back, enumerating again all the dangers we had before so amply discussed. But with the same earnestness did I expatiate on the evils of slavery, and enumerate the advantages which would result from our success. And how was success to be gained without exertion!

My reasoning at last succeeded, and fearing his resolution might fail if I were in the water first, I prevailed upon him to descend the rope. When he gained the water, the end of the rope became entangled about his foot, and he gave a kick to clear it. I trembled. The sound, increased by my fears, seemed like the plunging of a grampus, but the noise was drowned by the surrounding storm. As soon as he was clear, I slid softly down and slipped into the water without the smallest noise. I glided by the ship side, which I kept touching with my hands, thus gaining an idea about how fast the tide was carrying me. After I thought myself clear enough of the ship, I struck out, and in a moment or two came up with Patterson. I found him very ill. In his struggles to clear himself, he had swallowed some salt water which made him sick, and when I overtook him I found him vomiting. I encouraged him by all the means in my power, and when he had finished vomiting, side by side we proceeded cheerily along. I had practised swimming much more than my companion, and could therefore proceed with much more ease and expedition. I amused myself swimming around him relating anecdotes and singing, etc. When he became fatigued, we took each other by the hand and drifted slowly along until he covered the strength for further exertion.

When we were two or three miles from the ship, we were excessively alarmed by hearing the sound of human voices near at hand, and almost immediately observed a boat from shore standing towards the *Ceres*. We saw she must pass within a few fathoms and were overwhelmed with dread and terror, expecting nothing else than to be picked up and taken back, where we would have met with the most rigorous punishment, and probably been put in irons as long as we remained in harbour.

We did not swim out of the way lest our motions betrayed us, so had no other resource but to remain still and trust to providence. As she approached, our alarm increased and we tried to sink beneath the surface, but were prevented by the buoyancy of our bladders. Fortunately, she was rather to windward, and the belly of the sail hanging over the lee gunwale no doubt in some measure sheltered us from observation. What was also in our favour was that the crew seemed intent on some subject of debate, which continued as long as the boat was distinguishable. It may here be asked, had there been no apprehension of steering the wrong course? We had not. We possessed the most excellent compass, none other than the large comet of 1811, having frequently observed that it lay precisely over the point of land we wished to gain.

After many a trial to feel ground, Patterson claimed with joy, and in the words of Archimedes, 'I have found it! I have found it!' I was almost afraid to try lest I should be disappointed, but seeing him standing at rest, I let down my feet and found ground at little more than three feet. The shore was very shelving, for when we first gained the bottom we could scarcely observe any traces of land, and we had to walk about three-quarters of a mile before we gained the beach. On reaching it, we threw ourselves on our knees in united thanks to that being who had brought us deliverance, and to implore further guidance and fortitude.

Advancing up the beach, we saw a light, and crossing a field or two saw it proceeded from a pretty large house standing alone. A board resembling a sign was fixed over the door, but we could not read the inscription. On knocking, a person appeared at the window and demanded our business. We feigned a story of distress, but this made no impression on him. He told us in a surly tone to be gone, that it was past midnight, and at that time he would not open his door for any person whatsoever.

We tried another house with a light, but no better success. We left these houses to try to retrace our steps to where we landed, but missed our way. We soon, however, gained the beach at a different and much better place, a snug little cove in which a considerable number of small boats were lying. At this, we were overjoyed, and already anticipated completion of our project to gain the Essex shore and proceed to Maldon. After searching through a number of the boats, we found one seemingly Dutch-built, that had a small sail and a couple of oars on board. We slipped her painter, and as the wind was southerly, we set sail and stood to the north-east as far as we could guess. We were very wet and cold, but getting out the oars and pulling vigorously soon brought us to a state of agreeable warmth

About an hour before daybreak, we touched ground and hauled a little more to the eastward, resolving to get as far along shore as possible before dawn. We heard the *Ceres* fire her morning gun, and had the happiness of seeing her hull down. It was our intention to land before sunrise and we made several attempts, but the shore was so shelving, that we could not get within half a mile of it. We therefore continued edging along, and as we did so, saw many vessels resembling light colliers bound to the northwards, but could not think of venturing out to any lest they should betray us. We could easily have coasted along to Blackwater River and got into Maldon that way, but were deterred from this by considering that our appearance might render us suspicious. Besides, when day broke, we saw our sail was a man-of-war's hammock, which would make us appear even more suspicious. About midday, we were fortunate enough to discover a small creek just wide enough to receive our boat. The water in this creek being pretty deep, the boat did not ground until her stern took the land, so we did not even wet our shoes. What became of the boat we never heard, but we left her in a very snug berth and well moored, and as her owner's name was painted on the stern, we hoped, and doubted not, that he would ultimately recover her.

After passing over a small earth mound, erected to keep the sea from breaking into adjoining fields, we found ourselves in a delightful meadow. The sun was shining, scarcely a cloud was to be seen, while the mild zephyrs, as they skimmed along the fragrant meadow, seemed to whisper congratulations into our ears. Everything around us tended to accelerate our spirits and we gave unrestrained scope to our feelings – leaping, rolling, tumbling and shouting. Had any sober man seen us he would undoubtedly have questioned the soundness of our intellects. We saw a farmhouse at some distance, where we found only one woman at home. The truth cannot always be told, nor could it be told here: we fabricated a story about shipwreck, with as few falsehoods as the case would admit. But with whatever care a falsehood may be fabricated, a thousand questions may be put which the utmost of human ingenuity could not have anticipated, so a further thousand falsehoods have to be uttered in support of the first.

But in this case, the woman into whose house we went was of a mild and kindly disposition, and more inclined to pity than to doubt or question. She herself had a son who followed the sea, and who had been several times wrecked, so that she now felt for us only a kind of maternal sympathy. She set before us what a well-stored pantry and dairy could afford, and pressed us to partake heartily. At parting she would accept no payment.

'Keep your money, my lads,' said she, with kindness upon us, 'You have yet a long way to go' (we had told her we were for the north), 'and you know not what you may need.' The gratitude excited in our breasts by this genuine English hospitality produced in us the most delightful emotions; emotions which the greatest monarch on Earth, possessed of unlimited power, abounding in riches, surrounded by flatterers, and wallowing in sensual pleasure, might well envy. We learned that we were about twelve miles from Maldon, for which place, after taking an affectionate leave of our hostess, we set out.

A luxuriant store of brambleberries by the road and a desire to avoid entering Maldon with daylight induced us to linger by the way, so we did not reach this place till after dusk. We readily procured a bed to which, after supper, we immediately retired, and soon made up for the last night's leeway.

23. Home once more: October 1811

As we could not both obtain a passage in the same vessel, I procured one to Sunderland, and Patterson went to Blyth. There was not much accommodation in the Sunderland vessel, and as she did not intend to sail until next noon, I slept ashore. The wind, however, sprung up fair during the night, and when I rose next morning I found to my grief and disappointment that she had left. The little stock I had brought ashore with me, all wrapped up in a black silk neckcloth, was aboard of her, and was now forever lost to me. But it was in vain to lose time in murmuring or complaint. I therefore immediately set out making further applications and on the same day, 17 October 1811, was fortunate to get a passage for my work in a brig bound for Shields, which was to sail the day after the one in which Patterson had now got his passage. Experience, says the proverb, teaches fools, and so it taught me, for I took very good care to sleep nightly aboard.

The brig being bound for Shields caused me no small alarm, for there were, at that time, no less than four different press gangs belonging to that port. I strove, however, to make myself as serviceable as possible on the passage and by this means secured the good wishes of the captain, who had two pretty good stow holes in his vessel, one of which he was kind enough to appropriate to my use. But even this could not dispel my fears. I knew the sagacity of the press in discovering stow holes, and what my fate would be if taken.

It was quite dark where we arrived off Shields, and we had, with a great many more vessels, to lie to until about midnight before the water was high enough to admit us across the bar. At high water, a signal was displayed from the shore, at which a great number of vessels pressed forward as if sailing for a prize. The hurry and confusion was truly astonishing. As there was very little wind, tacking was completely out of the question, and back and fill was the order of the night. Several ships had their boats out for the purposes of towing and making fast the ends of hawsers to other vessels at anchor. The sound of jib booms, figure heads, martingales, yards, and so forth, coming together, the stentorian voices of the pilots, the nautical 'Heave ho' of the mariners as they braced about their yards and hauled their bowlings, the rough, hoarse voices of the captains directing their boats as to what direction to pull; all this, added to the darkness, created a scene of inexpressible confusion.

Whether the press gangs were not on the alert that night, or whether there were more vessels arriving than they could succeed in boarding, I know not, but to my unspeakable satisfaction, none boarded our vessel. When our sails were furled, the captain called me into his cabin, gave me what I could eat and drink, tied up for me in a handkerchief some cold beef and biscuit, carried me ashore with him in his boat, and leading me through the most unfrequented streets got me clear of the town before daybreak.

Blyth, the port of my friend Patterson, was several miles northward of Shields, and somewhere about halfway between the two was the town, Hartley, where Patterson's wife resided, and where we had agreed to rendezvous. The owners of the brig in which I had had my passage resided in Blyth, and the captain, going to report to them, set out for Blyth and proved a good guide for me. When opposite Hartley, this worthy man, whose name I have unfortunately forgotten, but whose kindness I will never forget, bestowed on me, in addition to his former kindness, a small sum of money to help me on my journey. Though Patterson had sailed from Maldon a day before me, we had shot ahead of them, and at Hartley we had seen the vessel he was aboard entering Blyth harbour, and knew he was now on his way home

I soon found the house of his wife and knocked at the door. 'Pray', said I, 'is John Patterson within?'

'No,' said Mrs Patterson.

'Could you please inform me where he is?' She

looked at me with some degree of distrust and answered evasively.

'Do you expect to see him soon?' I then asked.

'No.'

I then told her to prepare for the reception of her husband, as he would assuredly be home in time to breakfast with her. I gave a brief sketch of what had happened to us since John Patterson and I had become acquainted, and just as I finished my narrative, in bounced Patterson himself to confirm the truth of it. I will not attempt to describe the meeting between Patterson and his wife, but leave it to be imagined by those who have felt the torturing pangs of separation from the object on whom all their affections are placed.

I remained two days and on the third, being anxious for home, I set out to make the journey on foot. I might have gone to Newcastle, whence a passage to Glasgow by the traders might easily have been procured, but I dreaded the thought of again passing through Shields, and I therefore exchanged clothes at Hartley, giving myself the appearance of a countryman.

I need not dwell on the particulars which occurred in my journey. They were such as will generally be experienced by travellers whose dress and appearance are not very prepossessing and whose purse is light. I passed through Morpeth, Wooler, and Kelso. As I approached the latter town, I saw a very elegantly dressed female before me. When I drew near I found to my surprise she was barefooted. The sight of flocks of birds and discoloured water was not to Columbus a more sure indication than this was to me of my approach to Scotland. I accosted her, and enquired the name of the town and river on our right. She informed me it was Kelso and the Tweed. My heart warmed at the sight. I bounded joyfully along the bridge and paid my bawbee[42] at the Scottish end of it, and leapt with ecstasy onto my native soil.

I slept in Kelso that night, and next morning (Sunday) set out by way of Galashiels, Peebles, Carnwath, the Lanark, etc., for Paisley, which I reached a little after ten in the evening, 30 October 1811, after an absence of eight years and three months.

I did not immediately, as might have been expected, repair to my mother's house, but slept in the Black Bull, that I might have time to settle the plan of my introductory visit. I arose early, and repaired towards my mother's house. I stood some time at the end of the street, and feasted my eyes with scenes that youthful familiarity had rendered dear to me. I then passed to the other end of the street, and stood and looked back that way, but still did not venture in. Then I strolled along the banks of the canal, about which, even then, I began to hope I might get some employment. Then my appetite reminded me it was time to lay in a supply. Calling at the sign of the Ploughman and his Team, Causeyside Street, I had some refreshment. Then, ordering pen and ink, I wrote a letter to my brother, sealed it, and went directly to deliver it personally. Knocking at the door, my mother opened it.

'Pray, Madam,' said I, 'Are you Mrs Hay?'

'Yes.'

'You have a son at sea called Robert?'

'Yes.'

'Then you are the person I want. I am acquainted with your son, who is now on his way home, but as he knew I was to pass through this town before him, he requested me to be the bearer of this letter.' I then handed her the letter I had recently written. During the short explanation, she had come more to the door and had examined me with the most scrutinising eye. Natural affection had begun to work on her from the moment she first saw me, and it had, by the time I delivered the letter, risen to such a pitch that she could no longer restrain it. She forced me into a chair while tears of joy to listen in her ride.

'Ye are him, sir! Ye are him.'

'No, my good woman,' said I, 'I know your son. I know where he is, and when he expects to be home, and if you will compose yourself, I will give you a full explanation.'

Meanwhile, my brother John and sister Jean, who had gone to another apartment to read my letter, returned and gave it as their opinion that I was not their brother. My mother continued positive so that after persisting a little longer, but to no purpose, I rose up, threw my arms about her neck, and exclaimed, 'Yes, mother, I am indeed your son.' I now had as much difficulty to persuade Jean and John that I was their brother, as I had before to persuade my mother I was not her son. They examined me minutely, but traced no resemblance to their absent brother, and it was not until I mentioned several circumstances that no one else could know anything about that they became really convinced. We then embraced with great fervour and indulged freely in those exquisite joys that are experienced in near and dear relations after a long separation.

After being so long accustomed to an active life, I could not think of applying myself again to the sedentary business of the loom, and as nothing else appeared I went to school. My mother was very indulgent when I solicited her for the means of acquiring navigation. She immediately complied but I saw, however, that it was with some reluctance, she being uneasy at the thought of my going back to sea, wishing me rather to learn bookkeeping or some other branch that would have a tendency to keep me at home, but unwilling to oppose my inclination, lest it should be the means of making me depart.

But her fears were unfounded. I trust I have seen and learned enough to avoid and despise that pettish humour that makes some people so unhappy in themselves, and so troublesome and disagreeable to others.

I attended the schools through the winter, learning navigation and bookkeeping, and improving my knowledge of arithmetic.

In the spring of 1812, the trade on the Ardrossan Canal commenced. On 1 April, I obtained the place of steersman, and a few days after that, of captain in one of the trading boats. I continued in this situation until March 1813, when I was promoted to the office of clerk and storekeeper, the office I presently hold. In the autumn of 1815, I became acquainted with, and on 11 June following became united to, that woman who is now the part of my joys and cares.

When I consider for whom this narrative is intended, my children, I do not feel as inclined to expatiate either on the last mentioned event, or to dwell on the qualifications of my partner. I will dismiss this subject in a few brief sentences. She possessed then neither beauty nor fortune, but as I myself possessed neither, I had no reason to complain of the want of them on her part. These, however, I was always of opinion are by no means an indispensable prerequisite in the completion of happiness. She had a pair of excellent hands, an amiable disposition, and an agreeable temper, and indulged, moreover, a strong desire to promote my comfort and happiness. What more could I desire? In her company the five years of intervening space, during which we have been blessed with temporal prosperity and excellent health, have glided along in a happy, even tenor of uniformity. Little addicted to company, I spend most of my leisure in company with my books. From them, blended with occasional attempts at composition, I derive much amusement and perhaps some instruction.

I do not expect, however, that if my days are prolonged, such happiness will continue to distinguish them. I am yet but thirty-two, and thousands have there been in the world who, at that age, scarcely knew what trouble was, yet whose after years were marked with distress, adversity, and anguish. Man, we know, is born to trouble, and who is so presumptuous to expect exemptions from this universal law. Whatever measures of distress may be mingled in my future, I hope my Creator will endow me with the fortitude to bear such with resignation, that He will restrain me from every vice which is hateful in His sight, or injurious to my neighbours, that He will incline my heart to the cultivation of virtue and piety, and that He will furnish me with that sacred armour which alone can enable me to sustain the attacks of the last enemy without terror, apprehension, or dismay.

Paisley, Tuesday, 6 November 1821.

Notes

1. Quoted in Whitely, J H, *Wesley's England* (London: Epworth Press, 1943), p.81.
2. For readers interested in this debate, plus a list of other contemporary lower-deck accounts, a convenient summary is provided by Rasor, Eugene L, *The Seaforth Bibliography: A guide to more than 4,000 works on British Naval History 55BC–1815* (Barnsley: Seaforth Publishing 2008), p.216-226.
3. Hay, M D (ed.), *Landsman Hay: The Memoirs of Robert Hay 1789-1847*, p.188. By this time 'Boy' was a formal rating replacing the earlier 'Servant', although the high proportion of youngsters in the Navy continued to be assigned largely servile duties. The 'Landsman' of the book's title is actually the lowest rank of Seaman. Able Seamen were the most proficient, competent 'to hand, reef and steer', the elite of the ship; Ordinary Seamen were semi-skilled and useful for many tasks, but not usually aloft; the remainder, Landsmen, were regarded as little more than muscle, to tail on a rope, heave at the capstan, or perform any other mundane function as ordered. In more general use it applied to anyone who made his living on land – the opposite of 'seaman' – which gives the book title a double edge.
4. The sum would not have been paid out but kept 'on account' under the control of an officer who would doubtless dispense it for his own benefit, so this apparently 'paper' loss was very real.
5. Pemberton, C R, *Pel Verjuice* (London: Scholartis Press, 1929), p.9.
6. Ibid., p.94.
7. Ibid., p.144.
8. Hay, p.51.
9. Ibid., p.63.
10. Ibid., p.82-3.
11. Smollett, Tobias, *Roderick Random, Miscellaneous Works*, vol. I (Edinburgh: Stirling & Slade, 1820), p.223.
12. Hay, p.96.
13. Ibid., p.120.

14. Ibid., p.121.
15. Ibid., p.129.
16. Ibid., p.134.
17. Hay says March, but it was actually February.
18. Hay, p.190.
19. Ibid., p.232.
20. Ibid., p.247.
21. The exact figures are given in Lewis, Michael, *A Social History of the Navy 1793-1815* (London: George Allen & Unwin, 1960), p.134.
22. Lurting, Thomas, *The Fighting Sailor Turn'd Peaceable Christian* (London: J Sowle, 1711).
23. Dickens, Charles, *Barnaby Rudge* (London: Waverley edition, nd), Introduction.
24. Hutchinson, J R, *Press Gang Afloat and Ashore* (London: Everleigh Nash 1913), p.6.
25. Dickens, Charles, *Oliver Twist*, (London: Waverley edition, nd), Chapter 51.
26. In pre-decimal currency, 12 old pennies (d) equalled 1 shilling (s), and 20 shillings made one pound (£). The annual income for the Hay family would have been around £20 at a time when farmworkers and general labourers earned about £35-40 a year. Skilled textile workers might have earned twice that sum, and clergymen, for example, £250 pa, according to Williamson, J G, 'The Structure of Pay in Britain, 1710-1911', *Research in Economic History*, 7 (1982), 1-54.
27. Sowens – a dish made from oat husks and water, similar to porridge.
28. A guinea was the sum of 21s, that is £1 1s.
29. Tib's Eve – named for a non-existent saint, this is a colloquial term for 'never'.
30. *The Sailor's Word-Book* (1867) states that brab is 'the sheaf of young leaves of the Palmyra palm . . . from which . . . plait for hats is made'. In other words, Robert has been bought a triangular straw hat originating from foreign shores to replace his local plaid headgear.
31. According to the *Oxford English Dictionary*, 'stingo' is slang for strong ale or beer, but the mention of sugar cane would imply that the sailor's wife was carrying rum.
32. John Hamilton Moore, *The Practical Navigator, and Seaman's New Daily Assistant* (London, 1791).
33. Gunter's scale – a ruler used in navigational calculations, named after the mathematician and astronomer, Edmund Gunter (1581-1626).

Notes

34. According to *The Sailor's Word-Book* (London, 1867), lob-scouse was a mixture of salted meat, biscuit, potato, and onion, chopped finely and stewed together.
35. A kid was a bucket or tub.
36. Negus – hot drink of port, etc.
37. Pismires – ants.
38. To bouse (or bowse) up the jib – nautical slang for drinking alcohol.
39. The *Flying Dutchman* – a legendary ghost ship reputed to haunt the seas around the Cape of Good Hope.
40. Mother Carey's chickens – stormy petrels.
41. In other words, he was intoxicated by alcohol.
42. Bawbee – a Scottish halfpenny.

SEAFARERS' VOICES

A new series of seafaring memoirs

The lives and practices of our seafaring forbears have receded into the distant past, remote but also of fascination to a generation to whom the sea is now an alien place. This new series, Seafarers' Voices, presents a set of abridged and highly readable first-hand accounts of maritime voyaging, which describe life at sea from different viewpoints – naval, mercantile, officer and lower deck, men and women – and cover the years 1700 to the 1900s, from the end of the Mediterranean galleys, through the classic age of sail to the coming of the steamship. Published in chronological order, these memoirs unveil the extraordinary and unfamiliar world of our seafaring ancestors and show how they adapted to the ever-demanding and ever-changing world of ships and the sea, both at war and at peace.

The first titles in the series

For more details visit our website
www.seaforthpublishing.com